Your Towns and Cities

Stockport
in the Great War

Dedication

To Elsie Plant (suffragette and family planning clinic pioneer) of Woodsmoor, Stockport, and her three daughters: Aileen (nursery school head and traveller); Roma (business woman and retail owner); Joyce (writer, teacher and philosopher); and to all those people of Stockport who made the ultimate sacrifice in the 'war to end all wars' 1914–1918.

Your Towns and Cities in the Great War

Stockport
in the Great War

Glynis Cooper

Pen & Sword
MILITARY

First published in Great Britain in 2016 by
PEN & SWORD MILITARY
an imprint of
Pen and Sword Books Ltd
47 Church Street
Barnsley
South Yorkshire S70 2AS

ISBN 978 1 47383 378 4

A CIP record for this book is available from the British Library

Printed and bound in England
by CPI Group (UK) Ltd, Croydon, CR0 4YY

Typeset in Times New Roman by Chic Graphics

Pen & Sword Books Ltd incorporates the imprints of
Pen & Sword Archaeology, Atlas, Aviation, Battleground, Discovery,
Family History, History, Maritime, Military, Naval, Politics, Railways,
Select, Social History, Transport, True Crime, Claymore Press,
Frontline Books, Leo Cooper, Praetorian Press, Remember When,
Seaforth Publishing and Wharncliffe.

For a complete list of Pen and Sword titles please contact
Pen and Sword Books Limited
47 Church Street, Barnsley, South Yorkshire, S70 2AS, England
E-mail: enquiries@pen-and-sword.co.uk
Website: www.pen-and-sword.co.uk

Contents

✦

Acknowledgements

Thank you to Stockport Local Studies for allowing me to study the source materials for this book; to Roni Wilkinson, commissioning editor, for moral support; to the long suffering design and editorial staff at Pen & Sword, who take so much trouble with each manuscript; and to my family for their tolerance when I am engrossed in writing a book.

Introduction

❖

Stockport, which now lies within Greater Manchester, has changed a
great deal in the 100 years since the outbreak of the First World War.
Today it is a Metropolitan Borough Council that covers Stockport
Town, Cheadle, Gatley, Cheadle Hulme, Bramhall, Marple, Mellor,
Compstall, Bredbury, Woodley, Romiley and Hazel Grove. In 1914
Stockport Town consisted of the areas or former villages of Cale Green,
Edgeley, Heaviley, Heaton Chapel, Heaton Mersey, Heaton Moor,
Heaton Norris, Portwood, Lancashire Hill, Shaw Heath, Adswood,
Brinnington, Reddish, Davenport, Woodsmoor, Cheadle Heath and
Offerton. Reddish and the Heatons were quite recent additions to the
growing town. In 1914 the other townships now covered by the
Metropolitan Borough Council were very separate entities with their
own councils and, in some cases, were in different counties, so this
book will simply focus on Stockport Town as it was in 1914.

CHAPTER 1

1914

❖

Stockport lies at the junction of the River Tame with the River Goyt, which merge to form the River Mersey. There had been a settlement here since at least Anglo-Saxon times. In early medieval times there was a motte and bailey guarding the ford over the River Mersey, although by 1535, according to John Leland, an antiquarian in the time of Henry VIII, this castle was in ruins. It was finally demolished in 1775. Until the mid-eighteenth century, agriculture, growing hemp and a small rope-making industry were the main forms of occupation. From 1732 – 1770 a number of successful silk mills were established along the Mersey using machinery copied from that used in Italian silk throwing. But by the early 1800s, cotton manufacture had become the main industry. The hatting industry, which had been established in Cheshire and Lancashire since the sixteenth century, also really developed during the nineteenth century when Christies moved to Stockport in 1826. Rope-making continued in the town, along with the advent of iron foundries and engineering works. Before disappearing under a medley of mills, motor roads and myriad terraced housing, the countryside in and around Stockport was very pretty with woods, meadows, hedgerows full of hawthorn, elderflower, brambles and dog roses, bordering the two rivers. But in 1844, Friedrich Engels described the town as being 'renowned as one of the duskiest, smokiest holes in the whole of the industrial area', and by 1914 little had changed. The town was large, grim and dirty, full of dark mills, blackened chimneys

Buxton Road, Stockport c1910.

and cramped squalid housing. Its inhabitants were hardworking and stoical, many of them used to hardship and deprivation. But, despite their difficulties, they had a cheerful sense of humour. When war was declared on 4 August 1914, they faced it with courage and resilience.

The Great War, as David Lloyd George said, was fought primarily on grounds of money, trade and business interests, whereas past wars had tended to be fought over territory, principles and religion. Germany and Austria-Hungary were prepared and comparatively wealthy countries who believed that 'might was right' and that they would therefore win the conflict. Countries like Britain, France and Belgium were caught completely unawares. All of them initially underestimated the power and resources of Germany, Austria-Hungary, and the Ottoman Empire, which entered the war on the side of Germany. The battles of Gallipoli and the Dardanelles were disastrous for the British, who failed to understand they were dealing with a large, disciplined, well-equipped Turkish army instead of a bunch of indiscriminate snipers. However, what Germany and her allies failed to understand in turn was the utter determination of their opponents that the kaiser would not win.

Stockport, although a thriving, bustling and politically aware community, seemed to underestimate the gravity of the European situation. Instead, the local papers reported complaints that many MPs were 'tired of Lloyd George' and there was criticism of his latest budget, especially as the purchasing power of the pound was falling and this had caused industrial unrest. The Plural Voting Bill then failed to make it through the House of Lords. This meant that people who were affiliated to a university or had homes in two different parliamentary constituencies could still vote twice, or even three times, in any election. The burning issue of the day, however, was the Home Rule Bill, which advocated that Ireland should have self-government but remain British. The idea of Home Rule had been put forward by Gladstone half a century earlier in an attempt to reconcile Irish nationalism with being a part of Britain. This was so strongly opposed by the Conservatives and Ulster Unionists, it was feared civil war might result. At the end of July 1914, a palace conference was held at Buckingham Palace to try and resolve the Irish Crisis, and the king himself became involved. The conference failed to find a solution and, in their rage and frustration, the Conservatives and Ulster Unionists branded David Lloyd George's government as one of 'mess, muddle, Marconi and madness!' There was very little time or newspaper space for the European situation.

War was declared on 4 August and the first edition of the *Stockport Advertiser* to appear after this date was on 7 August. The first intimation of the war came on page 6 after two pages of advertisements, followed by the weekly story, gardening advice, the children's corner, parochial news and a 'shocking theft of cucumbers'. The paper was then at pains to explain Sir Edward Grey's attempts to avoid the conflict. He had negotiated at length with Germany but the Germans insisted that France and Belgium should co-operate with them or be annexed. Britain had a treaty of alliance with Belgium so the Germans tried to persuade Britain to 'sell the neutrality of Belgium'. Sir Edward Grey refused point blank to countenance this offer, but even then the British Government was uncertain that this would lead to war and dithered, although they should have been alerted to the real intentions of Germany and Austria from correspondence between the two countries relating to Serbia. The kaiser believed that Britain was 'bitterly divided politically and seriously disturbed industrially', and thought that realistically there was very little prospect of the country entering into a war against Germany. Bearing this in mind he 'imposed his policy of bluff, bluster and oppression' on France and Germany without appearing to understand that such a war would be bound to involve Belgium and Britain. It is said that privately the kaiser got on rather well with his cousin, King George V. If the two men had ever discussed the situation it is hard to believe that the kaiser would have thought as he did. It is more likely that German intelligence-gathering was at fault and they had simply failed to realise how firm and united the British could be in confronting a common enemy.

Reaction to the declaration of war was swift. Stockport wakes week that year was scheduled for 8 – 15 August. Factories, workshops and businesses closed down for one week a year to allow their workers a chance to escape the daily grind for a few days. Many had saved hard all year for a cheap excursion to Blackpool or Southport to recharge their batteries, but excursions and train services were summarily cancelled so thousands decided to save their money and stay at home. The mayor warned working folk to 'look to their savings'. Several local shows were cancelled although sporting fixtures continued. Local employment disputes and strikes were quickly settled so that the coming struggle would see everyone united together. 'No man can tell what miseries and disasters we may have to face by being dragged into a European war,' said one politician gloomily, not realising just how much of an understatement he was making. On 9 August, five days after the declaration of war, the local 6th Battalion of the Cheshire Regiment deposited their colours in St George's Church on Buxton Road, where they would remain until the regiment's return, and left

ST. GEORGE'S CHURCH, STOCKPORT.   COPYRIGHT.

ST. GEORGE'S PARISH CHURCH IS THE FINEST MODERN CHURCH, NOT BEING A CATHEDRAL, ERECTED
IN THE UNITED KINGDOM. THE CHURCH IS 180 FEET LONG & 75 FEET WIDE ACROSS THE NAVE AND
AISLES. THERE IS A PEAL OF 10 BELLS ABOUT THE SAME WEIGHT AS THOSE OF CHESTER CATHEDRAL
THERE IS AN OAK ROOF OVER THE NAVE & AISLES. EXQUISITIVELY CARVED. THE REREDOS AND FONT
ARE OF UNPOLISHED DERBYSHIRE ALABASTER. THE CHURCH IS BUILT OF FLECKED RED RUNCORN
SANDSTONE. IT HOLDS 2,000 PEOPLE. THE WHOLE COST OF CHURCH, SCHOOLS AND VICARAGE
TOGETHER WITH ENDOWMENT. WAS THE GIFT OF THE LATE GEORGE FEARN. ESQ J.P.
IT WAS CONSECRATED ON FEBRUARY 25TH 1897 BY DR. JAYNE. LORD BISHOP OF CHESTER.

St George's Church, Stockport c1914

Stockport to go to war. Two hundred men from the Stockport National Reserves also offered their services and Stockport Lacrosse Club set up a Home Defence Company. Lord Kitchener was appointed secretary for war, much against Lloyd George's better judgement, and the great recruiting drive began.

In Stockport recruitment was brisk and men queued enthusiastically to enlist in the recruitment offices on Churchgate. The plan was to teach the Germans a short sharp lesson and be back home in time for Christmas. This illusion did not last long and by September, enthusiasm was visibly waning. The Germans were part of a Triple Alliance, which also included Austria-Hungary and Italy, although Italy was supposedly neutral in the war. This Triple Alliance would later be joined by the might of the Ottoman Empire. Britain, France, Belgium and Russia were on the opposing team. At first it looked as though Germany and her allies might be the stronger protagonists, but the British Dominions hastened to the aid of the mother country. Troops from Canada, Australia, New Zealand, India and South Africa joined in to support Britain and her allies, while the king declared that the Royal Navy fleet was 'a sure shield of Britain and her Empire'. News of early naval victories strengthened this assertion. The first land battle, resulting in a Belgian victory at the Battle of Liège, also strengthened morale, and recruitment for the Cheshires improved considerably.

The Cheshire Regiment was originally part of an infantry regiment raised by the Duke of Norfolk in 1689. It was composed of militiamen, who were professional soldiers, and, from 1859, by volunteers who had other day jobs but attended rifle meetings and summer camps in their own time. The two groups were united in 1908 and the Volunteers formed the 4th, 5th, 6th and 7th Battalions of the Territorial Army. The 2nd/6th and 3rd/6th Battalions of the Cheshire Regiment and, in 1917, the 8th Volunteer Battalion, were stationed at the Stockport Armoury, in the Edgeley district of Stockport. The Armoury had been built in 1861 to house other fire power platoons and boasted a drill hall with a large yard, a commando post, rifle range, gun sheds, garages, and there was a band room in the tower. The 2nd/6th and 3rd/6th Battalions of the Cheshire Regiment Territorials had left for intensive battlefield training in Shrewsbury after war was declared, and a few days later the first of nine local volunteer training corps was formed in Romiley as a kind of Home Guard. Similar units were subsequently formed in Bredbury, Cheadle Heath, St Thomas's, Reddish, Heaton Mersey, Portwood, Heaton Moor and Offerton. They were then grouped together to form the 9th (Stockport) Battalion of the Cheshire Volunteer Regiment. The regimental headquarters stood on St Peter's Square in Stockport and administered the total of eleven volunteer battalions that made up this regiment. A full battalion usually consisted of 1,007 men, of whom thirty were officers.

An intercession service was held at St Paul's in London and Canon Alexander declared that 'ancient preserves of courage, loyalty, patience and dogged solution should be called upon [in] the nation's supreme crisis'. Canon J. C Jack of Stockport followed up this theme at Stockport Parish Church by preaching a sermon on the Battle of Armageddon. Recruitment drives and rallies were held in Stockport and a number of doctors and some chaplains were called-up. A Heaton Norris dentist offered free dental treatment for all enlisters, and soldiers were given free rides on the tram services. The newspapers did their bit for propaganda as well. 'Germany to be crushed' ran one headline. 'British forces fought splendidly' ran another. Drummer J. Lynch from Hollywood in Stockport, nicknamed 'the Drummer of Mons', told his 'thrilling story' of life on the battlefield.

Lance Corporal Herbert Pearson from Ducie Street wrote to his local vicar from France in the late autumn of 1914, his optimism and cheerfulness to the fore:

> *All classes of men* […] *have only one object* […] *the absolute annihilation of the Allemand* [German] […] *death holds no terrors* […] *they* […] *refer to it as "gone west".*

He gives the Territorials a great deal of praise and goes on to say:

> *We are now at our third station* […] *snow and frost reign supreme* […] *a lot of our men are quartered in barns and*

*stables with only one blanket [...] it is going to be a big
struggle [...] I understand we are being reinforced with
Japs [...] tobacco was issued to us yesterday [...] French
cigs and tobacco are horrible and to have a good smoke
of English tobacco is delicious.*

The immediate effects of the war were felt in Stockport as much as
anywhere else, if not more so, in the staple industries of cotton, hatting
and lace. The cotton trade was especially badly hit. Imports of cotton
bales slumped from 77,488 in 1913 to just 6,370 in 1914. Most cotton
mills were forced to shut down through loss of supplies and skilled
workers enlisting. Vernon Mills had 75% spinners idle. Leigh's Mills
and the Portwood Spinning Mill managed to keep going but on reduced
hours. The hatting trade was also badly affected. All local hat shops
closed down and Christies had to go on to three-quarter time working.
Coal exports ceased. This should have meant a surplus of fuel at home,
but much of the coal was requisitioned by the army. Trade and markets
were lost overnight with Germany and Austria when war was declared,
and bills remained unpaid. There was a problem for the banks when
nervous customers began withdrawing their deposits and the bank rate
rose to 10%. Stock markets closed. There was panic buying and
hoarding of food. The price of flour, butter, bacon and eggs rose sharply
as middlemen withheld stocks to force prices up even higher. Warnings
were issued against profiteers but seemed to have little effect.

Austerity and economy at home was preached in order to conserve
resources. A bill was passed in the House of Lords against privateering,
which caused sugar and bacon prices to fall slightly. Higher meat and
bread prices were said to be completely unjustified, but that did not
stop unscrupulous dealers freezing meat to force up prices. Despite
lower prices, sugar was rapidly becoming in short supply; particularly
as many would not accept alternative types of sugar to the favoured
lump sugar – a teaspoon-sized portion of sugar in the shape of a small
lump. Granulated sugar seemed to be especially frowned upon. Some
of the suggestions for cheap food were almost inedible. Newspapers
printed suggestions for frying scones from cold solid lumps of porridge

Armoury Square, Shaw Heath c1914

or substituting small pieces of turnip for slices of pineapple in fruit jellies, and an alternative recipe to the vegetables that usually accompanied meat and potatoes was given. Cooks were advised to boil up stale bread, potato peelings and old vegetable leaves together and then mash the result through a sieve. This would form a nutritious puree and could replace green vegetables. The troops did not have to suffer these unappetising suggestions, as the bulk of the food eaten in the trenches was bully beef (canned corned beef), bread and biscuits, and the infamous Maconochie army ration stew.

The Maconochie brothers were from Lowestoft in Suffolk but emigrated to Fraserburgh near Aberdeen to open their food factory. The stew was supposedly a meat and vegetable ration made from beef, potatoes, carrots, onions and haricot beans. Often it had to be eaten cold and this was described as a 'culinary perversion'. Army cooks, trying to be economical with limited supplies, made a cheaper version that was a thin soup of potatoes, carrots and haricot beans with turnips replacing the beef and onions. This was described as 'a man killer' when eaten cold. There was also an unfortunate side effect. Turnips and haricot beans eaten together produce lots of flatulence in the stomach and the effect on hundreds of marching men is unimaginable.

The loss of jobs in the cotton and hatting industries, coupled with the loss of the family breadwinner as men signed-up to enlist, left many families without means of support. Stockport Corporation paid allowances to the wives and families of reservists in its employ who were called-up. Christy's paid 10/- (about £50) to the wives of employees called-up plus 1/- (£5) per week per child under 14. Spinners and Weavers Associations paid out similar amounts to dependents of their members. Short-term, these arrangements were sustainable. Long-term they were not going to be viable because, with the downturn in business and the wartime economies, the funding was simply not going to be available. The council decided that an employment register might need to be set up, listing both those unemployed and the jobs available, so that the two might be matched together. In the meantime, Stockport War Relief Committee was established by Stockport Trades Council, and local war fund distress meetings were organised, although there were complaints at the lack of worker representation on these committees.

In the first three weeks of its existence the Stockport War Relief Committee dealt with 1,256 applications. Six hundred and seventy-five were made by men and 581 by women as heads of families without support. Assuming an average of at least four people per family, this meant that around 5,000 people were in immediate need of financial support. The government also paid a small separation allowance through the post office to the wives and families of soldiers and sailors, but this was, at best, inadequate, especially as rents also rose sharply.

There were voluble protest meetings about rising prices. One such meeting in Houldsworth Square, Reddish, attracted over 200 people. Bredbury Council held urgent meetings to discuss the question of relief. Stories of hardship and deprivation abounded. Children were badly affected and by October, over 2,000 children were going to school hungry. In 1906, the Provision of Meals Bill had been passed to enable local authorities to feed deprived children. Many felt that this discouraged independence and enterprise while others warned that

Town Hall, Stockport c1914

children don't learn well on empty stomachs. Stockport had not taken advantage of this bill before the war but, with the cotton and hatting industries now virtually stagnant, the thinking changed. By the end of October, public canteens were providing at least 2,000 children with breakfast and dinner (the term dinner referred to the midday meal in Northern England at that time and still does in several places). Potato pie was a hot favourite with the children, and 100 years on many northern pubs still serve potato pie suppers on quiz evenings or for charity events. Other dishes included haricot soup, pea soup or lentil soup, which were served with a dumpling, or there was Irish stew or potato hash to ring the changes. The meals were served in basins not on plates, and most of the children ate ravenously.

A month into the war, Queen Mary established a Work for Women scheme to help those who had lost their jobs as a result of the war. They would be paid 10/- a week (around £50) to knit and sew clothes and comforts for the troops.

Subsequently she broadened its aims:

- to employ women and girls in mending and darning
- to train women and girls in hand ironing
- to establish training schools in domestic economy and cookery for women and girls

Queen Mary's workrooms were established first in Central Hall in Stockport and then in the larger Masonic Hall. Rent was charged for the use of these rooms although the amount was lower than usual. The mayoress of Stockport, Mrs E. Potts, also set up a workroom on similar lines to Queen Mary's scheme. Her aim was to train women and girls to make clothes for children and poorer people from old discarded clothing. Some complained it was a threat to trade, but she retorted that it was no threat at all because the recipients were either too poor or too young to buy clothes anyway. There was also a Stockport school for mothers established in the Forresters Hall on High Street following the same principles as the Manchester maternity centres. It had already been recognised that the war 'will take the best of our manhood', and Stockport had one of the highest infant mortality rates in the country. This, however, was much reduced by the education of mothers on feeding and how to care for their infants. Poverty, poor living conditions and lack of proper sanitation and hygiene were still major problems, but understanding what was required helped mothers to minimise the risks.

Women also played a large part in the work of the Red Cross with nursing, knitting and fundraising activities. There were three ways in which the Red Cross offered assistance to the war effort:

- financial help
- provisions, equipment and staff for convalescent homes nursing wounded soldiers
- clothing, hospital requisites, medical comforts, etc, for troops serving on the front line

Stately homes and country seats like Brabyns Hall in nearby Marple,

Bramhall Hall and Lyme Park, both a few miles down the road, were turned into Red Cross convalescent hospitals, as well as the Wesleyan Schools in Heaton Mersey. Nurses from Heaton Chapel and Heaton Moor gained their qualifying certificates from nursing work undertaken in the Heaton Mersey hospital. Some went to Stockport Infirmary, which had initially set aside twenty beds for wounded soldiers, where the staff carried out their work with 'mercy, skill and love'. Although there was still great resistance in many professions and industries to women working, nursing had always been seen as women's work along with childcare, cooking, cleaning and sewing or knitting. However, a Women's Emergency Corps was established in London, which would soon spread to other parts of the country. The *Stockport Advertiser*, upon enquiring about this newly formed corps, was told that women were now acting as clerks, conductresses and even chauffeurs and that a female chauffeur was 'a splendid type of woman who proves her efficiency by driving most skilfully, avoiding accidents, and being apparently equal to any emergency'. A hundred years on, the jury is still out on the question of the skills and efficiency of female drivers.

Towards the end of August came news of the first Stockport war casualty. Edward Lees of Edgeley was a radio operator on the merchant ship *City of Winchester*, which was captured by a German cruiser in the Indian Ocean on 6 August. Although there was no definite news of the crew, there was a strong probability that they had been landed in Mozambique, and this gave hope to the Lees family that their son had survived. There had been a lull in recruiting so, in mid-September, there was a huge demonstration at the Armoury emphasising the 'justice and righteousness of the British cause' in a great show of patriotism with stirring speeches on 'the duty of able bodied men to fight for the cause'. Although the speaker admitted that the 'British race are lovers of peace', it was necessary to crush the German principle of 'might is right'. It was pointed out Stockport's population was about 125,000 and that from this number the town should be able to provide at least 5,000 recruits. Lord Kitchener had already secured 500,000 enlisters nationally, but now admitted he needed the same number again. The Cheshires were 'in the thick of fighting' in France and had lost eighteen

Wellington Road North, Stockport c1914

officers at the Battle of Mons. Fired up with beliefs in family honour and national pride, men queued up once more to 'take the king's shilling'. Numbers for the Cheshire Territorials were now almost complete, so recruiting was for a new reserve battalion. A pals battalion was proposed for Stockport as well and the Mayor, T. W. Potts, contacted the War Office with this suggestion. A Stockport shop assistants corps was also proposed, following the example of Stockport Lacrosse club, whose corps members were now serving in Egypt. The news from the Front was still optimistic. 'Many guns and prisoners taken' trumpeted one headline following a German retreat while another condemned the Germans as 'uneasy and cowardly'.

From the third week of the war the *Stockport Advertiser* had decreased its size from twelve pages to eight pages to help the war effort by conserving paper supplies. Page eight was devoted to news, casualties, updates and analyses of the war. Bell & Co of Hempshaw Brooks Brewery in Stockport had already suffered a fall in trade due to the huge increase in beer duty, which was causing great resentment among drinkers. So it was then proposed that Stockport pubs should close early as their contribution to war economy, but there was fierce resistance to this move and the pubs stayed open. Postal deliveries were restricted to three a day: at 7am, 1.30pm and 6.30pm. A hundred years on even this reduced service sounds like luxury. Willow Grove Cemetery, keen to do their bit, donated two graves for foreign soldiers or sailors who died of their wounds in Stockport hospitals and convalescent homes. Construction of roads was undertaken to provide work for some of the unemployed as well as improve the means of transport. These included the widening of Banks Lane, Dialstone Lane and Warren Street.

Despite the war ordinary life and concerns dominated much of the local news. There were serious issues like the depressed state of the cotton industry, the mistreatment of pit ponies at Bredbury Colliery, and the death of Thomas Kay JP, ex-mayor of Stockport and chairman of the Stockport Infirmary Committee. Well-respected in the town, he was a keen educationalist and also the founder of the Maia Choir. Then there were vexatious issues such as vandalism in Reddish Park, when five youths were fined for 'misuse of the swings', and bitter protests

Naval battle of Falkland, Atlantic Ocean 1914

1914... Combat naval des Falkland (îles anglaises, océan atlantique) La fin du Charnhost" vaisseau amiral allemand

1914... Naval battle of Falkland (English isles atlantiques océan). The end of the Charnnost' german admiral ship   (E&D)

from Reddish Vale Golf Club about the bad smell caused by a new sewage drainage and cesspool installation system. The Theatre Royal on St Peter's Square tried to lift everyone's spirits a little by putting on *Hindle Wakes*, which was termed 'the play of the century'. A Stockport girl, Anna Bethell, played the principal part of Fanny Hawthorn.

The question of Irish Home Rule was still being hotly debated. However, Kaiser Wilhem, who had believed the Home Rule controversy to be a bitterly divisive issue, was astonished by the coalition of Conservative, Unionist, Liberal and Labour politicians who laid aside their differences to govern their country during the war. It was a unity for which he had not bargained and it dashed his hopes that Britain, distracted and diverted by its internal and industrial problems, would ignore Germany's military aims and manoeuvers.

Belgian refugees began arriving in Stockport needing care, assistance and accommodation. Woodville in Reddish was offered for this purpose, followed by Hythe House in Heaton Chapel and Woodlands in nearby Woodley, the latter rent free. Stockport Co-operative Society gave a concert in aid of the Stockport Belgian Relief Fund, which then stood at £100.14s.7d (around £10,100) from subscriptions and was used to pay for food, clothing and rent. The Belgians had terrible and heart-rending tales to tell that appalled those who heard them and strengthened resolve that the kaiser was not going to win this conflict. Recruiting continued steadily and an appeal was launched by the mayor for blankets for soldiers. An additional request was made by the navy for high, water-tight boots for sailors. There was also a Cheshire and Lancashire fundraising initiative for tobacco for the troops and, as part of that, E. Robinson & Sons, tobacco manufacturers in Stockport, offered to supply forty-eight cigarettes and 2oz (about 57g) of tobacco for each 6d (just over £2.50) given.

The autumn of 1914 was a grim and gloomy time of painful adaptations to the demands of war. By mid-November, the *Stockport Advertiser* had begun a weekly roll of honour in the paper for those killed in the fighting. There was plenty of news about the Cheshires. They had faced 'a baptism of fire in France'. Recruitment drives were ongoing and regular lectures were held about the war, its causes and effects. Despite this, the December newspapers were full of Christmas shopping and excursion advertisements. There was a Christmas appeal to send gloves to the Cheshires for Christmas. There were also Christmas fund and parcel appeals by the mayoress and an appeal by Princess Mary, the daughter of King George and Queen Mary, for Christmas presents for the troops. Families could send individual parcels, but it was inadvisable to send fresh foodstuffs that might go rotten before a parcel reached its recipient. Tins, jars, fruit cakes and even a bottle of whisky were acceptable. Christmas presents and comforts could also be included. In addition, the mayoress had appealed for donations of one undressed doll. The dolls would be dressed by the relief workrooms she had set up and distributed at Christmas to the children of soldiers, sailors, Belgian refugees, and those receiving relief. The Christmas card trade suffered, in spite of the Royal Family making it known that they would be sending more cards than ever, but the Christmas trade in gifts and edible treats was brisk. Robinsons announced that 5,732 sixpenny pieces had been donated so 46,080 cigarettes and 1,920oz (over 54kg) of tobacco were dispatched to the troops. For Christmas entertainment, Stockport Operatic and Dramatic Society produced *Geisha* at the Theatre Royal. There were a number of concerts given by local choirs, and the mayoress arranged a performance by the Minnehaha Minstrels at the Town Hall. Despite everything, however, it was 'a war darkened Christmas' and a sad time for those who had already lost someone.

CHAPTER 2

1915

⬦

The ongoing hostilities of war provided a temporary boost for the cotton trade. The industry had never really recovered from the cotton famine during the American Civil War and trade had been on a roller coaster in the half-century since that war had ended. Although continental and other markets were lost overnight when the war began, the demand for khaki and blue military uniforms soared and, overall, 1914 and 1915 saw the largest turnover and profits for the industry in its history. It was a swansong, however, and sadly for the cotton trade was the beginning of the end. One of the main problems was that many skilled male cotton operatives were enlisting in the forces. In Stockport, over 12,000 men, nearly 10% of the total population, signed-up to serve their country in the first year. Mills in Portwood and Reddish Vale suffered particularly badly. Sheds were forced to go onto short-time working and the Stockport Spinners Society was paying out £350 (over £35,000 at current values) per week in unemployment benefits. Women and young teenagers could have been trained to fill the gap to a great extent, but initially there was strong resistance from the unions to female workers doing skilled jobs that were reserved for men, and equally strong resistance to seeing children working in the mills again. The hatting trade suffered a similar decline, although there had been a downturn in trade for the preceding eighteen months due to export difficulties as a result of cheaper alternatives in other countries, increases in freight carriage and insurance problems. Continental trade markets were lost overnight with the advent of war. Skilled male workers in the industry signed up for military service and many workshops closed. However, the felt hat trade remained buoyant. The idea and design of felt hats had been copied from the popular Austrian models. They did not require the same amount of work or skill to produce, and women and girls were chiefly employed in the manufacture.

Women and girls were also employed in the millinery and dressmaking trades, but appreciable numbers were leaving to train as nurses. The number of men enlisting in the forces was creating a demand for female labour outside traditional female areas, and women were rising to the challenge. The National Union of Suffragettes suspended their activities for the duration of the war to take charge of women's relief work, employment for women, nursing the wounded and caring for Belgian refugees.

Private Joseph Keable of Portwood wrote to his former schoolmaster that 'Belgium is in ruins'. A local composer, Ralph Sanders, wrote a song called *Queens of the Red Cross* in tribute to the 'sweet sisterly nursing care' given by the women. However, agriculture proved to be a closed industry because farmers were implacable in their opposition to female labour, believing that women were totally unsuitable, untrained and generally unemployable. Ironically, at this time, Reddish Shakespearians and Amateur Dramatic Society chose to perform Oliver Goldsmith's well-known comedy *She Stoops to Conquer*.

Zeppelins had embarked on what one writer described as 'a mission of murder', and their aerial bombardments caused widespread terror. Invasion was now seen as a real threat. Heaton Mersey had a 'newly founded and highly creditable' civil defence corps, which had recently opened a shooting range. Other areas followed their example. Local boy scouts formed a defence corps and there was a Stockport women's defence corps as well whose members numbered about 300. Captain Moir, a Stockport man, was given the task by the Cheshire Territorials of recruiting 200 cyclists for the Welsh Division Cyclists Cheshire Company. Bicycles and uniforms would be supplied.

David Lloyd George, however, was concerned about the enemy within as well as the enemy without. He discovered that the nation was spending more on drinking than on munitions for the war and his reaction was one of scathing contempt as he labelled working men 'drunken shirkers'. This was unfair and unjust because many worked long hours in appalling conditions and heavy drinking wasn't confined to the working classes. Lloyd George's stance, however, was that if the Germans invaded, the population would need to be reasonably sober in order to defend themselves properly, and there was no real argument with this point of view. There had been about a 12% rise in cases of drunkenness in Stockport, from 483 in 1913 to 554 in 1914. Lloyd George, to his credit, didn't single out any town or city for particular criticism. He simply saw the problem as a general one that needed addressing.

In January, the military authorities had already insisted that pubs and clubs were not to sell any alcohol to serving soldiers or sailors between the hours of 9pm one day and midday the following day. Under the Defence of the Realm Act (DORA), which was passed shortly after war was declared, the military and judicial authorities were empowered to take whatever action considered necessary to help the war effort and defend the nation. Consequently, further new licensing restrictions were introduced on 12 April. Pubs and clubs could not open before 10.30am and had to close by 10pm on weekdays and 9pm on Sundays, and station buffets were prohibited from selling whisky or brandy, although they could sell lower proof alcoholic drinks within the designated licensing hours. These were followed by quite prohibitive restrictions in October. Opening hours were reduced from the original 19½ hours (5am – 12.30 at night) to 5½ hours a day (12 noon – 2.30pm and 6.30pm – 9.30pm), and a 'no treating order' implemented, which meant that people could not buy alcoholic drinks for others. Beer, wine and spirits were now quite heavily taxed and it was ordered that all spirits should be diluted with water.

DORA also instigated restrictions in lighting at the same time to make it harder for the Zeppelins to see targets during night-time raids. At this point there wasn't a total blackout order due to working, trading and safety aspects, but street lamps were ordered to be partly obscured. Manchester chose to darken the top of its street lamps so they would be less visible from above, while giving pedestrians below some much needed illumination of the streets. Stockport always kept a keen eye on what Manchester did and townspeople often seemed to feel they were in competition with their neighbouring city, comparing the two places endlessly and attempting to re-assure themselves that they had done as well as, if not better than, Manchester. However, the lighting restriction situation now descended into farce as Stockport decided how to partially obscure its street lights.

The town had no option but to obey the DORA restrictions, although they did it their way and obscured the lower part of their street lamps. Consequently, people struggled and fell in the darkened gloom of the streets while from above clusters of pretty glowing lights could be seen from afar, prompting one wit to comment that while Manchester was expecting attacks from Zeppelins, Stockport was clearly expecting attacks from submarines. The last word unwittingly came from pupils of local Claremont College, whose spring production was *Comedy of Errors*.

In March, the local paper reported that 'the forcing of the Dardanelles is one of those bold and dramatic strokes which cannot fail to thrill […] and impress the whole world' and that 'tottering Turkey will be staggered'. There was also 'fierce fighting in France', and by Easter Stepping Hill Hospital and the infirmary could no longer cope with the numbers of wounded soldiers needing treatment. Stockport resolved this problem by turning nearly half its schools into military hospitals. Greek Street High School for Girls was the first to be taken over in May 1915. It was followed by Alexandra Park Council School in Edgeley, St Georges School, Vernon Park School, Hollywood Park Council School and, finally, North Reddish School. In order that the children's education should not suffer too much, Stockport Town Council adopted a four-shift system. All the children were to be transferred to other schools so that one school building would contain two schools and the pupils would be taught in rota. The first school's pupils would have lessons with their own teachers from 8.30am –

10.20am and 1.00pm – 3.50pm. The second school's pupils would have lessons with their own teachers from 10.30am – 12.35pm and 3.15pm – 5pm. Alexandra Park children went to St Matthews School on Chetham Street while St Georges' pupils attended Cale Green Council School. The infants from Hollywood Park and Vernon Park had slightly different hours and were taught from 9am – 12 noon and 2pm – 4pm. It was not an ideal situation but it did mean that all children could be taught the three Rs (reading, writing and arithmetic) plus some basic history and geography knowledge. Evening schools were also run in North Reddish, St Peter's, Christchurch and Edgeley Parish Church for those who had left school but wanted to learn further skills. Classes were well-attended with numbers ranging from 92 to 280 on average. The one area of education in which Stockport was found lacking was schools, institutions and resources for those children with special needs, either physical or cerebral.

Wounded soldiers from Ypres were being cared for at Stepping Hill and the infirmary struggled to cope with the number of soldiers suffering from the effects of the chlorine gas now being used by the Germans. Chemical warfare was something new. It was very much resented by the troops and one newspaper castigated the enemy, using the words of the Duke of Wellington in 1815, who wrote of the Germans that 'the earth never groaned with such a set of murderous infamous villains'.

Heaton Chapel Red Cross provided an extension at the Military Auxiliary Hospital on Cavendish Road in Heaton Mersey, and there was also the Ralph Pendlebury Military Hospital established in Pendlebury. The total number of military patients was now some 700 – 800. Appeals were made for funding for all the military hospitals and for items such as gramophones and motor cars for convalescing soldiers. There were regular outings for all military convalescents, accompanied by nurses from the Nurses' Home in Greek Street, mainly to Torkington Golf Links, where a variety of entertainment followed by tea was arranged. In July, Stockport also organised a France Day with the aim of aiding the equipping and maintenance of hospitals for the wounded all over France.

St George's Schools Military Hospital, Stockport c1915

Recruitment had been slow over the Christmas period of 1914 and by Easter 1915 the newspapers were full of military news, recruitment drives and pleas for patriotism. Cheerful letters from the Cheshire Territorials on the 'light side of the war' were published in the Stockport newspapers alongside 'thrilling tales' from the Front. There were heavy casualties among men from Stockport, both in the Dardanelles and on the Western Front, and more men were needed to replace them. However, in the Stockport area there was also a number of pacifists and conscientious objectors who did not agree with the war or with fighting, and who flatly refused to join the armed forces. While there was some sympathy for their beliefs at home, their views were not shared by the men serving abroad who felt that pacifists and conscientious objectors only had the freedom to hold such beliefs because others were fighting and dying to allow them this freedom. Lord Derby started a national recruiting scheme and travelled around the country to speak in its support. He visited the Armoury in Edgeley and around 8,000 Stockport men attested under the scheme. The Cheshire Volunteer Regiment had already made remarkable progress with nearly 10,000 members, but losses were heavy, especially in the

Recruiting tram, Stockport c1915 (courtesy of Stockport Local Studies)

Dardanelles, and many more recruits were needed. Stockport sergeant, H. Payne, appealing for yet more volunteers to sign up, wrote a parody of the new song *It's a Long Way to Tipperary*, aimed at those he described as 'shirkers at home'.

On the road from Tipperary
There's a place that's vacant still;
There's a rifle lying silent,
There's a uniform to fill.
True, at home they hate to lose you,
But the march will soon begin
On the road from Tipperary
With the army to Berlin.

Food and fuel prices were rising and there was a meat shortage. Beef was expensive and it was becoming increasingly difficult to obtain all meat supplies. Stockport butchers now closed every afternoon except Fridays and Saturdays. The reasons for the price rise and shortage of meat were mainly due to the government purchasing 25,000 – 32,000 tons of the imported meat every week to feed the troops leaving only 7 tons to be distributed and sold at home. Some thought the British ate too much meat anyway. 'The English housewife spends her money to less advantage than her French sister,' wrote one local newspaper. 'Less meat would be a good permanent rule. One meal per day is enough [...] less beef and more lentils on our menus.' Rising gas prices were another cause of serious concern. There had been a three-year upward trend and the price of coal was now 'amazing'. At the same time there had been a decrease in prices obtained for residuals, or by-products, which had long been an important source of income for gas companies. Finally, there had been a decrease in gas consumption due to industry cutbacks and stoppages as a result of the war. Stockport councillor Mr F. Plant stated that 'the cost of coal is reaching famine prices', which he believed was 'mainly due to the 15.5% war bonus paid to workers and the 25% dividend taken by the proprietors'. As he saw it, the industry faced two enemies, 'Huns and unscrupulous traders'. He also complained that it was notoriously difficult to obtain colliery balance sheets. Another problem was that large numbers of miners were enlisting and there was an acute labour shortage in the mines. Electricity prices were also rising due to increases in production materials. The rateable value of Stockport borough had increased from £576,934 (£40,340,000.00) to £585,092 (£40,910,000.00), mainly as a result of the cessation of building operations since the beginning of the war. The war had placed a heavy burden on the town and rates rose accordingly. Mainly due to increased costs and decreased demand, £10,102 (£712,600) was lost from the gas, tramways, electricity and waterworks undertakings of Stockport Council. The education department was warned it would have to cut back, but there were problems. The department had spent £3,600 (£251,700) to provide breakfasts and dinners for 2,000 children in the last year, but had only initially set aside £600 (£41,950) for doing so. If children were to receive a decent basic education and sufficient food in school the options for making cuts were limited. One option was not to give teachers a pay rise, or to pay them the war bonus, which many other employees received. As another option, the finance committee proposed to reduce the amount the education committee was spending on evening schools. However, the new central library was thriving and book circulation was the highest recorded to date. Charles Dickens' 'great free school', as he termed public libraries, was clearly providing learning, information and recreational sources in place of other means.

There had been a problem with a severe shortage of shells almost since the war began. Lord Kitchener, however, insisted that the army had sufficient ammunition. Finally, after the British lost the Battle of Aubers Ridge on 9 May, it became more than abundantly clear that this was not the case. This resulted in a great deal of political wheeling and dealing, which brought down Asquith's government, and at the end of May a new coalition government was appointed in the wake of the shell crisis. H. H. Asquith was still prime minister, but David Lloyd George, formerly chancellor of the exchequer, headed a new munitions ministry. Sir Edward Grey was the foreign secretary and Andrew Bonar Law was the minister of the empire. A war cabinet was also appointed,

Stockport in the Great War c1915

which consisted of one Labour, eight Conservative and twelve Liberal members. Lord Kitchener remained minister for war, although he lost control of munitions and their production, and Arthur Balfour was the first lord of the admiralty. Eight million shells a month needed to be produced, because a 250,000 shells were being fired on the battlefields each day. David Lloyd George, as minister of munitions, set about meeting these targets, emphasising the paramount importance of the work. In north-western England, mills that were disused or doing very little business were converted into munitions factories.

Premises on St George's Road in Stockport that had once been a sawing and planning mill were converted and enlarged for production of munitions. Hornsby's gas engine works in Reddish was also converted. Stockport had an engineering industry, which was thriving despite the war. The call for munitions workers needed the skills and experience of engineers as well as large numbers of less-skilled workers for the more mundane jobs. Wages were high compared to other industries, and Stockport was very responsive to the call for munitions workers. Both men and women applied and registration progressed rapidly. Benefits for working mothers include a nursery and a works canteen. As it was a war work project, it was covered by the Munitions of War Act 1915, which meant that employees could not leave without the consent of the employer, and also made it extremely clear that strikes were not permitted. At this time, with the exception of Russia, Britain experienced more strikes than anywhere else.

A national campaign of thrift and economy began because government spending was running at £3million (£209,800,000), but the daily return through taxes was only £750,000 (£52,440,000). A 'gigantic loan' funded by the past, present and future savings of the nation was needed. The new government then 'devised means whereby all classes of people may share in assuring the success of the further loan by the state for the prosecution of war, and in expressing in practical fashion their sentiments with regard to the war'. Around £910,000,000 (£63,630,000,000) was needed for this purpose. Folk could purchase 5s vouchers (about £17.50), which would carry 5% for every completed calendar month. When the vouchers amounted to £5 (almost £350), they could be changed in a £5 war bond at any post office. It was a clever way of asking the public to contribute yet more funds to the enormous amount required for the war coffers. Determined to include everyone, especially the working classes, the war loan scheme was eventually closed to those investing £100 (almost £7,000) and upwards but left open to smaller investments of 5s (£17.50) to £5 (£350). Wakes savings clubs were abandoned and the money put into war loans. In any case, there would be no excursions or cheap fares to discourage travel and save on fuel, so for most the wakes would be a home holiday.

There was an appeal to women and older children to help with the harvest, as was the custom in France and Flanders. However, war or no war, the prejudice among Cheshire farmers, to whom Stockport Farmers' Association belonged, towards women doing any kind of farm work was so great it proved impossible to implement female help. Sexism and anti-female prejudice was far more pronounced in Britain than in France, Russia or Poland, where women were considered comrades. In New Zealand, Maori women, who were expert shots, had been mortified to discover that they were prevented from enlisting in the British Army purely on grounds of an accident of birth. In Stockport women were not even allowed to use the main gate of the munitions

Recruits returning from route march to the Armoury 15 June 1915 (courtesy of Stockport Local Studies)

factory in Reddish but were forced to use a small side entrance to emphasise their lesser status. Female tram conductresses in the town were pushed around and verbally abused by local men. How incidents like those must have irked the suffragettes, who had bravely put aside their own aims and ambitions to help wholeheartedly with the war effort.

At the end of July, Stockport town council instigated their preliminary preparations for taking the National Register in Stockport, as laid down under the terms of the National Registration Act passed earlier in July. This was mainly in response to the fact it was widely felt that young single men were not doing their duty and enlisting. So far, 844,000 married men with families had enlisted and were costing the nation £25,000,000 (£1,748,000,000) a year in separation allowances and pensions. Consequently, on 15 August, all men and women aged 15 – 65 years were to register at the address where they usually lived. This differed from a census in that each individual, and not the head of the household, had to register on their own form. Twenty-nine million forms were issued nationally for this purpose. Men had to complete a blue form and women had to complete a white form. Separate card indexes were then compiled for men and women. Indexes for both sexes were in two groups —one for single people and one for married people. Each group was sub-divided into occupations. There were forty-six groups for males and thirty groups for females. These were then sub-divided again into age groups, eight groups for men and six groups for women, before being filed alphabetically. From this information two further indexes were compiled. Pink forms were completed for all men aged 18 – 41 years and green forms for people with secondary occupations. Registration certificates were then issued to each person and recorded in a ledger. It was a mammoth exercise and, many suspected, merely a complicated and intentionally confusing way of ascertaining how many men were of military call-up age, where they lived, any particular skills they had and whether they were already engaged in war work. In Stockport, local teachers undertook delivery and collection of the forms. The town was divided into 295 districts and enumerators each had about 100 houses in their remit. There was a £5 (£350) fine for anyone who refused to complete the forms or who gave false information.

Shortage of labour was becoming a big problem for the cotton mills. Stockport Ring Spinning Mills alone had lost 50% of their staff through men joining the armed forces. In addition, China and India had stopped buying cotton goods for some time. Giles Atherton, the chairman of the Ring Spinning Mills, believed that the stocks of these countries must now be low and soon the orders would come flooding in. The reality was very different. The two countries had actually bought up a great deal of British machinery during the 1880s and the 1890s. No one had thought to question this as the profits were rolling in, but both China and India were in the process of setting up their own cotton industries. Japan and the US followed suit. The war was also having a disastrous effect on the cotton trade because the government had failed to look for alternative supplies of raw cotton in the wake of the German bombardment of merchant shipping. Apart from India and the US cotton was grown in Egypt, Andalucia, Turkey and Australia. However, this did not prevent strikes and disputes in the industry throughout the war. Wages were not particularly good and certainly did not keep pace with rising prices. Stockport dyers went on strike where the men ceased work for a week to enforce a claim for a 2/- (about £7) war bonus, and refused to accept the company statement that it could not afford to pay bonuses as well as allowances to enlisted employees. In September, at Palmer's cotton mills in Portwood, 500 employees resumed working after a strike that had lasted since July. These stances, and those of others in the production of cotton, irked their former comrades who were now serving in the army. Local newspapers were sent abroad as reading matter for the troops and to keep them in touch, and they wrote letters for publication on a number of subjects. Although they could sympathise with the problem of rising prices and low wages it was pointed out that soldiers earned a good deal less than cotton workers, they could not strike and, unlike their comrades safely at home, faced danger and death every day in the trenches.

Stockport saw itself as a garrison town but there were very different parts to Stockport. There was the mill-town and the humble cramped working-class dwellings down near the rivers, the Cheshire Regiment and the Armoury, and the more wealthy areas such as Woodsmoor, Davenport and Heaton Norris. The Cheshires made unusual requests for melodeons and chess sets to be sent to the Front and the *Stockport Advertiser* printed the following tips for 'economy'.

- no private house building to be undertaken
- no unnecessary home improvements to be made
- no luxuries to be bought
- reduce the number of servants
- meals to be only two course instead of five courses

There were pleas for old potato stocks to be eaten or planted for new potatoes, and for flower gardens to be planted with cabbage, onions, globe beet, spinach and lettuce. The war budget affected everyone and 'imposed additional and unprecedented burdens' on the population. Fifty percent extra duty had been levied on tea, tobacco, cocoa, coffee, chicory and dried fruits, and 33.3% had been levied on motorcycles, cars, cinema films, clocks, watches, musical instruments and plate glass. Luxury goods were clearly less affected, but the government, then as now, had an eye to the main chance and taxed the commodities that were popular (some would say essential), and which everyone bought. Tariff forms were hotly contested by the free traders lobby, but the government needed to raise a lot of money within a short time to continue supporting the war. Milk prices also rose sharply, but there were discrepancies and anomalies according to which areas were affected most, particularly on the fringes and in the poorer quarters of Stockport. There was also much discussion as to the allocation of Stockport gas profits. The general view was that the consumers should not benefit but the shareholders, who were the town's ratepayers. Further problems were caused by a shortage of labour at the gasworks as men left to take up better paid munitions work. Pleas for as much economy as possible sat uneasily alongside advertisements for 'costumes for morning and evening wear; golf skirts and motor coats' in the *Stockport Advertiser*. The cost of the war in terms of men and munitions was the subject of an important debate in the Commons. The war loan was referred to as 'silver bullets', and it was generally accepted that money was going to be the decisive factor in this war while Lloyd George maintained it was a war being fought on business grounds rather than on principles.

Recruiting was at an all-time historic low in the town by early September, and casualties in the Dardanelles and on the Western Front were heavy. A recruiting campaign in mid-September met with a very moderate reaction. There was still great controversy about married men going before single men and young men holding back to take older men's employment after they had enlisted. The younger men replied that many of them had family commitments as well. They were looking after aged parents or siblings with dependants. That was true to some extent, but there was still a lot of artful dodging going on. It was the same everywhere and Lloyd George privately admitted to himself that,

AFTER THE BATTLE

Western Front c1915

in the end, compulsory conscription would have to be made law before the army would get the numbers it needed. Then there was the problem of the pacifists and the conscientious objectors. The *Stockport Advertiser*, a very traditional newspaper, decided that all pacifists must be Labour Party members and all Labour Party members were pacifists. It was rather more complicated than that. There was a sizeable Quaker following in the town and Quaker beliefs involved pacifism. Fenner Brockway, a leading Quaker and a pacifist, lived in Stockport and would always give shelter and support to pacifists and conscientious objectors. Some were prepared to help with the war effort as long as it was in non-combat mode. Some refused point-blank and were often imprisoned for their beliefs. Others just ran away and lived off the land, mainly though stealing food from farms. It was usually felt that they brought shame and disgrace on themselves and their families. What they called principles, others called cowardice. Soldiers argued that if they weren't willing to fight and die for freedom from the yoke of living under the undemocratic rule of the German kaiser then no one would have the freedom to practice any of their beliefs. It was an insoluble problem and a very difficult situation.

The socialists were generally opposed to the war but, nevertheless, Labour organisations agreed to co-operate on recruitment matters. Lord Derby's recruitment scheme initially created a good impression in Stockport. Since the National Registration had taken place it was discovered that there were some 11,000 – 15,000 men in Stockport who were not engaged in munitions work. It was therefore resolved that every man not 'starred' (employed on war work) on the pink form as being engaged in war work should be personally canvassed. They were classified by age into forty-six groups: twenty-three groups for married men and twenty-three groups for young single men. It was agreed that the Derby Scheme canvassers should meet on 1 November to begin work and Stockport made detailed arrangements for up to 15,000 men to be canvassed as quickly as possible. Employers were reasonably understanding, although Lord Derby professed himself sympathetic to their needs. The king also made a personal appeal for enlisters. Nelson's dying words 'Thank God I have done my duty' became a kind of mantra for those attempting to persuade reluctant individuals to join the forces. Trafalgar Day (21 October) was still celebrated in Stockport.

Despite the labour shortages in the town 200 apprentices and journeymen from the 1,200 members of the hatters' union enlisted. Nevertheless, the divisive issue of married men versus single men caused controversy and opposition again and proper distinction between the classes of starred and unstarred (not in an exempted occupation) men was not clear in some cases, so a circular was issued to clarify matters. The *Advertiser* blamed the working classes, but it was not all their fault. There were middle class socialists and upper class conscientious objectors.

Helping to pay for the war was not the only call on the purses of Stockport folk. Rising prices of food and fuel as well as rising rents took their toll. Colonel A. J. Sykes MP raised the problem in the House of Commons of rapidly rising rents and accused profiteers of having a field day. It was beyond belief, he said, that the rents of enlisted men should be raised causing untold hardship to their families. In addition, there was the fundraising for wounded troops, the military hospitals, Belgian refugees, British prisoners-of-war, orphaned children, the British Red Cross, food parcels for those overseas, Christmas boxes for soldiers and sailors … the list was endless. In a single night, on 28 September, 350 soldiers were admitted to the military hospitals in Stockport. 500 wounded troops were equally distributed among the five schools that had been requisitioned as military hospitals. However, despite all the problems, people gave generously of their time and money. Pendlebury Red Cross Hospital raised £587.4s11d (over £41,000) in street collections. Joshua Preston endowed a bed at Stockport Infirmary in memory of Nurse Edith Cavell, who was shot for treason by the Germans because she helped 200 Allied soldiers escape from Belgium. Lifeboat flag days (the lifeboats helped the navy over fifty times and saved 334 lives in six months) in Stockport raised £390 (over £27,000). Cheshire farmers held a cattle sale and raised £10,500 (£734,100) for the British Farmers Red Cross fund, which was supporting hospitals in Serbia and Belgium. The Stockport farmers' share of that total was £1,500 (almost £105,000). Stockport also supported general appeals for ambulances to transport the wounded to the Anglo-Russian hospital in Petrograd, funds to be sent to Polish peasants for food, shelter, clothing and seeds, and to the Serbians for food, sustenance and shelter. Christmas boxes for the troops and food parcels for British prisoners-of-war were also well supported. The *Stockport Advertiser* opened a sixpenny fund for comforts and Christmas fare for wounded soldiers in local military hospitals. A sixpence was worth about £1.75 in today's money, and any number could be donated. The mayor, T. W. Potts, had recently been elected for a third term, and he organised a relief committee for 'the alleviation of distress and the municipal, industrial and social well-being of the town', supported by fundraising events in the town.

Christmas was a subdued affair. Everyone's thoughts were with the soldiers fighting at the Front and the sailors defending British shores and trade. Stockport's Theatre Royal reflected the general mood during the two weeks of Christmas by putting on the patriotic *It's a long way to Tipperary*, followed by the pantomime *Cinderella*. The *Advertiser* published its end of year review, listing changes and initiatives that had occurred on the Home Front during the past year. Prominent was the Derby Scheme and attestation. About 15,000 men in Stockport were thought to have finally attested their willingness to fight if called upon, but there were still recruitment issues and the question of compulsory conscription. The other major crisis had been the shortage of shells, which had resulted in the passing of the Munitions Act and the setting up of a munitions industry. Other changes had been either national or local, but they had all affected Stockport.

The cotton industry was depressed and there was a slump in hatting, both mainly due to shortages of labour and materials, although the engineering trades were doing well. The trams were also doing good business, especially as train travel was now restricted, although a sour note was introduced when male tramway workers were awarded a war bonus that was denied to the female tramway workers. There were shortages of meat, wheat, sugar, milk and coal. Rents, rates, gas, electricity, coal and food costs had all risen. Import tariffs had now been imposed upon a number of commodities followed by the inevitable price rises. DORA imposed licensing restrictions on pubs and clubs and lighting restrictions in the streets. The numbers of wounded men returning had risen alarmingly, so schools and large private houses were being turned into military hospitals. The cold bloody fingers of war had reached out and were now touching everyone at home as well.

CHAPTER 3

1916

❖

The big question on everyone's mind as 1916 dawned was that of compulsory conscription. It was obvious that Kitchener's endless demands for more men were not going to be met by those volunteering to fight. He had asked for 500,000 extra men and as soon as he had them he asked for another 500,000. The lack of munitions had clearly undermined British efforts during the first eighteen months of the war and casualties were high. The shell scandal was still fresh in everyone's minds despite Kitchener's pleas for it to be forgotten. Lloyd George knew that Kitchener was guilty, at best, of a serious miscalculation in his assessment of the munitions needed to win the current battles. He had also faced the fact that compulsory conscription would be the only way to obtain enough men to satisfy the voracious war machine. Consequently, Asquith introduced a bill for compulsory military service in January. Stockport's Labour MP, George Wardle, voted against the bill on the first reading and abstained on the second reading. The railwaymen, who Wardle represented, were vociferously divided in their opinions of his action. Wardle's Stockport colleague in the commons, the Liberal MP Spencer Hughes, missed the first reading but voted for the bill on the second reading, and the Military Service Act became law on 2 March enabling all single men aged 18 – 41 years to be called up for service in the army. This caused uproar and outrage at the injustice of being forced to fight when one had taken no oath to do so and also that married men were not included. While much of the country and parliament were full of patriotic fervour, many people still felt that the legal compulsion to fight might be a step too far. The House of Commons found itself in uproar over the question of 'compulsion or compromise'. David Lloyd George wanted compulsory military service for all men over the age of 18, the retention of time-expired men and a more vigorous combing out of single men from munitions factories and reserved occupations. He was supported in his views by Lord Derby, whose voluntary attestation scheme had met with only moderate success. The unionists and Labour members threatened to resign if these measures became law. Lloyd George, Andrew Bonar Law and Lord Curzon threatened to resign if these measures were not accepted. The coalition was now in danger of total collapse, which would necessitate a general election being held. Realising this would be a disaster, Lloyd George softened his stance and proposed that a general bill of compulsory military service be passed, but its compulsory powers would only be exercised when the numbers of voluntary enlisting by unattested married men fell below 50,0000 per month.

The House of Commons still felt that compulsory enlistment of single 18-year-old lads was no more justifiable than the compulsory conscription of unattested married men, but the differentiation was made more for parliamentary expediency than for any other reason. The heated debate over single men versus married men and compulsory conscription raged on.

At this point, the Easter uprising in Dublin took place. Irish republicans, trying to take advantage of Britain's pre-occupation with the war, rose up with the aim of ending British rule in Ireland and establishing an independent Irish Republic. The rising was quickly suppressed by the British Army, but it was a diversion they did not need and proved to be a wake-up call.

All attested married men between the ages of 27 and 35 (the final attestation groups of thirty-three to forty-one) had now been called-up and a new military service bill was drafted, which included all men between the ages of 18 and 41, the retention of time expired men, and the setting up of a new special reserve, which would train men for Home Front service.

The second Compulsory Conscription Act was passed in May, but there was still much opposition. Tribunals were set up to hear hundreds of appeals for exemption from all over the country and there were dozens of appeals in Stockport. However, very few were granted and certainly none to conscientious objectors or pacifists who used the teachings of Jesus, claiming that He had been the first conscientious objector, and the works of Tolstoy to support their case. The local Quakers had become alarmed by what they saw as 'military preparations for prosecution and prolongation of war', and they supported the conscientious objectors. Many pacifists and conscientious objectors did eventually agree to carry out non-combative duties or assist the Royal Army Medical Corps, but some, like Jehovah's Witnesses, absolutely refused to fight or to assist in any way and were often imprisoned for their beliefs.

Public scorn for conscientious objectors was now turning to rage and resentment and they were vilified by their friends, families and the newspapers. Patriotism was the word on everyone's lips and families like the Hollands of Reddish, who had seven sons fighting in the army, were held up as an inspiring patriotic ideal. Members of the clergy went to the Front, although for non-combative duties, and batches of unregistered vagrants were rounded up, fined, imprisoned for fourteen days, and then sent to fight. Meanwhile, the mayor managed to raise two battalions, the 145th and 155th East Cheshire Heavy Batteries of Heavy Artilleries, in Stockport. They left the town in a heavy blizzard at the end of March to complete their training before being sent out to the Front. It was also announced that the Volunteer Training Corps in Stockport had received official recognition by the government and King George V.

In order to do the jobs that men had been doing, women had been training for many occupations including clerical duties, tram conductresses, drivers, munitions work, retail and even engineering, in addition to their more traditional roles in nursing, teaching, child care and domestic work. However, not enough were volunteering or employed in agriculture. They were capable of being as good as the men and more were needed. Farmers were encouraged to employ them

Cheshire farmers near Great Moor, Stockport c1916

for milking cows, tending farm animals and increasing production of foodstuffs. Although their own wives and daughters probably did much similar work on the farms, farmers were unbelievably prejudiced against hiring female labour, especially for milking cows. The image of the English milkmaid has been perpetuated by various artists for centuries, but by the time of the First World War, all milkers had to be men. This, of course, affected milk supplies and deliveries in turn. Cheshire farmers, who included a number of Stockport farmers, were far more intransigent about female labour than some of their Derbyshire and Lancashire neighbours.

The summer of 1916 brought matters to a head. Extra labour was always needed at harvest time and traditionally sons, brothers, male relatives and friends helped out. By now there was an acute shortage of any male labour, but Cheshire farmers refused point blank to accept female harvest workers. There was a camp at nearby Handforth that contained nearly 2,000 German and Austrian prisoners-of-war. British prisoners-of-war in Germany were made to help with the harvest so the services of the Handforth prisoners was offered as free harvest help to the Cheshire farmers. They too were refused amid much grumbling that Germans weren't wanted on British farms. Lord Newton furiously condemned 'the prejudice, stupidity and ignorance in this country'. Then a band of itinerant labourers arrived from Ireland to earn money from working on the farms. They were refused work as well by Cheshire farmers on the grounds that the wages requested were too high. Time was now running out and finally, in desperation, the government was forced to bring back 1,750 fighting men from the Front for four weeks to help with the harvest. Cheshire farmers, who preferred their own sons to help run the farms and market the produce, had remained rigid in their methods, practices and prejudices to get their own way. Labour bureaux set up in Cheshire villages to cope with harvesting work were only allowed to supply male labour. The government, who had already been forced to repatriate experienced ploughmen from the Front to till the fields, regarded the situation as completely ridiculous and determined that within the next year, Cheshire farmers, including all the Stockport farmers, would not have any choice but to accept female farmhands.

In February it was announced that drunkenness had greatly declined in the Stockport area. The main reasons given were that large numbers of men were away and the effect of the new liquor restrictions. Others countered with allegations that secret drinking at home had increased and that women were drinking away their separation allowances. However, there was no evidence to prove that these things happened and, had it been the case, surely someone would have noticed that there were a number of drunken ladies about the town. Ironically, the Stockport Garrick Society began its season of plays with *The Merry Wives of Windsor*.

There were 301 licensed houses in Stockport. Unlike modern pubs and off-licenses, which sell all types of alcohol, these licensed houses specialised and sold just one or two types of alcohol. So there were ale houses, beer houses, beer off-licenses, spirit dealers, wine off-licenses and dealers. The population at this point numbered 126,040 and the licensed premises ratio worked out at 1:418. In addition, however, there were thirty-six music/singing/dancing clubs, which sold no alcohol, and fifty-four registered clubs, which could sell intoxicating liquor.

The wartime measures now began to bite harder, which made life even more difficult for many people. Reductions in education meant that voluntary and untrained teachers were now taking classes. However, it was considered better for the children to have some learning than none at all.

New lighting restrictions required all lights to be shaded, obscured or switched off from 1½ hours after sunset until half-an-hour before sunrise. Road repairs and maintenance became a problem and Stockport folk suffered weekly from serious accidents to pedestrians, several of which proved fatal. Some voiced concerns about safety and trade, but some even wondered if murder by Zeppelin could be worse than being run over and killed.

The earlier closing time of shops and the market were strictly enforced on the grounds that less sales and, therefore, reduced use of staff and utilities encouraged economy. The new licensing laws pleased tee-totallers and no one else. Inns were not allowed to sell alcohol before lunchtime but many still opened at 5.30am to provide tea and hot Bovril for mill workers and scholars.

Prices of food, fuel, milk, construction materials and even shoeing of horses continued to rise and the mayor appealed for economy in using coal. Average shopping bills had risen by 17% since the war began. There was a paper shortage as well as a shortage of raw materials for the cotton industry. The *Stockport Advertiser* limited itself to eight pages instead of the twelve pages it had run before the war, and only printed pre-ordered copies. Stockport Infirmary was suffering financial problems due to the numbers of war wounded needing treatment and the increased cost of commodities. To make things even worse the end of March saw blizzards 'trying to all living things, animal or vegetable'.

The war effort was proving incredibly costly to finance and another £420,000,000 was required. At current values this represents a staggering £24,850,000,000. However, even this sum did not cover the extras provided for the troops by the Stockport and District Comforts Fund, the costs of food parcels for prisoners-of-war, the entertainment for wounded soldiers, or the festive fare for those in hospital at Christmas. Concerts (like those given by Minnehaha or the brass bands in local parks) were frequently held and trophies from the Front were displayed alongside red collecting boxes.

Belgian flag days were held and the money raised was used both to care for Belgian refugees in Stockport and 'distressed Belgians in Belgium', a country that had been almost totally destroyed by the war. The Red Cross used flag day collections to provide bandages, medical supplies and field ambulances, and the YMCA held fundraising events to finance YMCA huts, which provided shelter and recreation for the troops. Most gave willingly, but not everyone was generous and Davenport Golf Club sued an Adswood farmer 'for allowing his vicious horses to damage the turf' during an event.

Shortage of labour was becoming an ever increasing problem and Cheshire Education Committee agreed to exempt children aged 13 to 14 from school so they could be employed on war work, providing they had obtained a certificate for at least 300 attendances at not more than two schools over the preceding five years. Juvenile crime, however, was increasing. The authorities put this down to a number of causes, which included absentee fathers, working mothers, a lack of discipline, revolts against restraints, the gulf in education between parents and children making children contemptuous of their parents, the general stresses of town and city life, the lure of street trading, earning too much money too young, and 'the influence of picture houses as the effect of some classes of moving pictures on the childish mind is not beneficial'.

Counter measures permitted as punishment for bad or criminal behaviour included whipping for boys up to 16 and the number of strokes to be increased to twelve. Parents were to be fined and ordered to pay for damage caused by their children. Empowerment of school teachers to punish errant children. Street trading to be prohibited for boys and girls under 16 and cinema attendances were to be restricted for those on probation.

After the war it was hoped more facilities and recreation grounds would be provided for children. The infant mortality rate was high at

204 per 1,000 births (a rate of almost 25% infant mortality), and the need for children to replace adult wastage in the war had never been greater. The Stockport School for Mothers helped a great deal to reduce infant mortality with its care for both mothers and small children and its teachings on food, hygiene and proper childcare. In 1907 the infant mortality rate in the town was 431 per 1,000, the figure approaching 50% of all babies born in the town, and in under ten years this had been reduced by half, although it was still far too high.

An incentive to have larger families was offered in the reform of annual tax rebates for each child under 16 in the family and the local newspaper lamented that 'more well born children were needed'. The birth rate had actually been increasing since the start of the Industrial Revolution but, as one writer put it, 'industrial civilisation demands sacrifices of babies' lives and decent living standards' and that 'the monstrous toll on victims has to cease'. Social reforms began with the mothers and children, but the country had more pressing matters on its mind.

Economies were now the order of the day and to make further savings on fuel and lighting the government decided to introduce the new Daylight Saving Act, which came into force on 21 May 1916 for the first time. The clocks were to be put forward one hour and this would remain so until the end of September, when the nights were starting to draw in, and the clocks would then be put back an hour. British Summer Time (BST), as it became known, is still in use today and there are currently arguments for BST to be made a year round fixture. BST was generally welcomed and Stockport Traders Association recommended revised closing hours for all traders so that everyone could benefit from the extended daylight hours and cut their fuel consumption. It was proposed that shops and businesses should close at 7.30pm on Mondays, Tuesdays and Wednesdays; that there should be a half-day on Thursdays, with 1pm closing; Friday closing should be extended to 8.30pm and Saturday closing to 9.30pm. Evening opening continues to be favoured in Europe, particularly in the Mediterranean countries, but, with the exception of supermarkets and out-of-town shopping centres, many shops and businesses in

Britain are currently closed by 6pm. It was agreed that local parks should be open an hour later for the duration of BST.

Further economies in other areas had to be made as well. Stockport Board of Guardians agreed to meet once a month instead of once a fortnight. Reddish reduced banking hours to 10am – noon daily from 1 June. Due to good economic housekeeping by Stockport town council, the rates were reduced by 2d in the pound (then 240d), although the main economies mostly affected roads and education rather than saving fuel on lighting. Even chickens found themselves affected by the tough economy measures when the government decided to relax poultry-keeping regulations on the condition that no roosters were kept.

It was also advocated that further provision must be made for maternity and child welfare as economies would seriously affect the generation that was going to replace the depleted war generation. Whitsuntide holidays were postponed for munitions workers and miners. Some felt the holiday should be abolished altogether as the troops got no holidays at all, but the cotton trade and the engineering workers turned a deaf ear and took their Whitsun holidays as usual. Rising food and milk prices continued to cause concern and many did not have much money to spend anyway.

Although the government tried to soften the hardships caused by the breaking up of homes when men enlisted, their wives, families and dependents still continued to bear most of the financial burden of moving and storage. Stockport was losing fighting men on an almost daily basis and the roll of honour published each week in the *Advertiser* grew longer. In addition to the Western Front, Gallipoli and the Dardanelles, there was also fighting in the East African jungles. Lord Kitchener, now the war secretary, made a series of speeches to rally the troops and on the services of the Volunteer groups, but he emphasised that problems of supply, money and manufacture of equipment were causing difficulties because the cost of maintaining the regular army was enormous. He then left to go to Russia for confidential negotiations but on 5 June his ship, HMS *Hampshire*, struck a German mine off the Orkneys and Kitchener was drowned.

Exclusive Post Card Edition   Active Service, No. 37

SHELL FIRE
One of the most remarkable photographs of Shell Fire ever taken. Three shells can be seen just as they have burst right over some houses.

Shellfire in France c1916

General Sir Douglas Haig took over the reins and it was under his leadership that the infamous Battle of the Somme was fought. Lloyd George was against the Battle of the Somme from the start. He believed that it would prove to be a disaster. A confident Haig told Lloyd George that he simply didn't have the necessary military experience and training to judge whether or not a battle would be successful and that he should stick to politics. The Somme would be a one-day battle that would teach the Germans a short, sharp lesson and regain territory for the Allies. To prove his point Haig decided to have the battle filmed by the early movie cameras, which would bear witness to military victory by the Allies and prove Lloyd George wrong in his belief that the battle would be a disaster. In the event the battle lasted for four months, over 1,000,000 men were killed or wounded, and tanks were used for the first time. Lloyd George's overview of the battle of the Somme was completely vindicated and led to some harsh recriminations from which Haig would suffer for the rest of his life.

This dreadful carnage still had to be financed and Lloyd George instituted a national war savings week and issued war savings certificates. He referred to the cash given to the war effort in this way as 'silver bullets'. The war savings week in Stockport began on 16 July, just a couple of weeks after the Battle of the Somme had begun, and there was a well-attended meeting in the lecture hall at the Central Library on 'silver bullets and savings' resulting in a tremendous drive to save a few shillings a week to invest in war loan stock or war savings certificates. Sacrifices small and large had to be made, the politicians said, as the public had not yet fully realised the acute need for war finance. However, many Stockport folk felt that the daily growing casualty lists and the continuing loss of loved ones were their sacrifices, both large and small.

Meanwhile, there was, literally, 'trouble at mill' in Stockport. Cotton workers' wages were low and the cardroom workers were pressing for an extra 5% on top of the 5% they had already been awarded. Prices were continuing to rise and, as they pointed out, the munitions workers were paid much better wages. Problems with coal supplies and shortages of labour prompted the miners and colliers who remained to put in a pay claim of time-and-a-quarter for working during the Whitsun holidays. Male tramway-workers were awarded a war bonus, which was initially denied to female tramway-workers. Through the local newspaper columns serving soldiers professed themselves a little fazed as to why there was all this squabbling about who earned what. Folk at home worked in comparatively clean, decent, safe conditions for more than a regular soldier's pay. Soldiers could not strike, did not have holidays and were daily facing death in the hell of the trenches. The munitions workers were not allowed to take holidays either because enormous numbers of bullets and shells were required at the Front. The prime minister, Herbert Asquith, said there should be no holiday atmosphere at home and appealed to workers in Stockport and other northern towns to postpone their traditional August wakes week. The cotton and hatting trades immediately announced their intention of defying Asquith's request and taking their wakes holidays anyway, but despite this, local holiday club savings withdrawals were well down on the previous year.

Lloyd George had long maintained that this was a war that was as much about profit as principle. There were those who were making money out of the war requirements and there were unscrupulous hoarders and black marketeers who withheld goods and supplies until prices were forced up. Stockport town council was deeply embarrassed when it was discovered that its own sewage works department had profiteered from a potato scheme. The committee had authorised that potatoes should be planted on an 8½ acre site. The total cost was £140.13s.0d (£9,870), but the potatoes were sold for £255.13.0d (almost £18,000), netting them a total profit of £115 (£8,000+). The average cost of growing a similar crop of potatoes was £2.10.0d (£175) while the price of potatoes was around £10 – £12 (£700-£840) per ton.

Bogus charities were set up, forcing the government to pass the War Charities Act to regulate raising money through bazaars, sales, entertainments or exhibitions, for purposes connected with the war. There were also concerted efforts by a number of people, mostly young men, to step into jobs left vacant by others who had enlisted and then using the labour shortage to force up wages by threatening to leave their jobs unless they were paid more money.

This was the enemy within and caused almost as much dislike and resentment as the Germans, the enemy without. In the middle of August, the Star Picture Palace on Higher Hillgate showed the very aptly titled film *Debt of Hate*. However, it wasn't just at local level that profit operated above principle. It was believed that after the military war had ended there would be a commercial war with Germany and that tariff reform and other measures needed to be initiated immediately to prevent the Germans from dumping goods in Britain after the war and then coming over to take the best jobs. Consequently, when the Germans offered peace proposals at the end of June to evacuate France, Belgium and Serbia within a week, they were regarded as bogus proposals simply designed to create indecision and division among the

Allies while committing Germany to nothing. Besides, it was felt that 'Britain did not yet deserve to win the war' and, in any case, committed business interests were not yet ready to end the war. Subsequently, it was decided to implement the measures of the June economic conference held in Paris by the Allies. These involved isolating the Central Powers (i.e. Germany, Austria-Hungary, Bulgaria and the Ottoman Empire) through trade sanctions after the war was over. This was of great concern to the United States because included in the plan were schemes for the 'subsidisation and government ownership of manufacturing enterprises' by the Allies (Britain, France, Italy and Russia) after the war and the division of the European markets between them. America had not entered the war at this point but it did not stop them from being aware of where the commercial interests lay.

There continued to be heavy casualties among Stockport men fighting on the Somme throughout the summer. Local churches offered what comfort they could to bereaved families, but grief hung heavy in the air. The prime minister's own son was killed at the Front during the summer and he empathised with the country's sorrow. Wakes week was a rather wet disappointment to many folk, although the rain did not affected the Cheshire harvest too much, but there was general discontent among the Cheshire farmers over the high prices of wheat and animal feeding stuffs.

The only signs of relative normality seemed to be the constant activities of the Boy Scouts and the regular bowling matches that took place between the various Stockport townships. Football and cricket seemed to have taken a low profile since the war began, but bowling retained its impetus.

The trades unions were as concerned about the ongoing industrial unrest as the employers and the government. At their annual congress they determined that the welfare of workers was dependent on four things:

- the constitution of the individual
- will and intelligence
- action of authorities
- local conditions

They concluded that the full co-operation of capital, management and labour was needed to ensure maximum working output. Welfare supervisors had recently been introduced into factories and it was noted that they were able to eliminate much 'discomfort and discontent' by taking an interest in existing individual employees and giving new employees a gradual induction into their new job.

It was realised that production was not necessarily facilitated by continuous overtime and it was decided that women engaged in moderately heavy work should not work more than sixty hours a week, while those engaged in light work should not work for more than sixty-two hours a week, especially in the munitions industry. This idea was confirmed when a new act on the health of munitions workers was passed and it was discovered that for men a 10.4% reduction in working hours led to a 13% increase in output and that the general output increased by 42% after working hours were reduced from 70.3 to 57 a week.

This may have worked well but it did not solve the problem of meeting the steadily rising costs of food and fuel with continuing wage increases and war bonuses. Railway workers had claimed, and were awarded, a double amount of war bonus. Calico printers were having a particularly tough time because they now faced competition from the US and Japan. The Near East markets were closed due to the war and similarly trade with India, China and Spain was restricted. Cotton spinners demanded a 20% increase in wages, which provoked a fresh crisis in the cotton trade. The TUC advised acceptance of arbitration but the cotton spinners refused because they were still dissatisfied after the last award. Cotton mills were also suffering because, already badly denuded of labour, their employees were to be combed out for further army recruitment. Their female labour was denuded as well because the women had gone into the munitions factories, as well as other occupations, where they could earn better wages.

Women were now working as tram guards, post women, clerks, helping wounded soldiers and making up Red Cross parcels of food, comforts and newspapers for the troops. There were still shortages in agricultural labour and employment of women on the land, although there had been 1,120 female volunteer applications to work on farms. Cheshire farmers were accused of 'selfishness rather than self-sacrifice' in refusing to accept female labour, and labelled 'stupidly slow' in recognising the value of women working the land. But the government stuck to its guns and registrars of the various village labour bureaux were ordered to either persuade or insist that farmers train women.

Cheshire County Council was condemned for refusing to employ German prisoners as labour on farms or the roads. The council retorted that it was fully justified in its protests at the issue of orders by government departments without being given opportunities for discussion or amendments. Besides, its farmers were uncertain about employing soldiers for agricultural work because of their uncertain abilities. The government view, however, was that the country was at war, conditions were very different to those of peacetime, and the council was behaving in a ridiculous fashion, as Germany was employing British prisoners-of-war on all classes of work. In response the council muttered darkly about 'far reaching dislocation when war employment was stopped and disbanded millions re-entered the labour market'. It was an impasse.

There were widespread concerns about the constantly rising price of milk and Stockport council attempted some sort of general regulation in areas within its jurisdiction for the price of milk sold, the amounts in which it could be sold and the number of daily deliveries allowed. The usual minimum amount in which milk could be sold was a quart (1.136 litres), and one delivery per day was allowed. Bredbury farmers, however, refused to listen and would not meet with the council. Not everyone, they argued, could afford to buy milk in quarts and everyone should be able to afford some milk. Consequently, they ran a morning delivery where milk was only sold in quarts (as per the council ruling) but they also ran an afternoon delivery where milk was only sold in gills, which was a quarter of a pint measure (0.142 litres). Discontent over milk prices continued for most of the autumn until finally, after a 'great deal of agitation', Bredbury and Romiley farmers reduced the price of their milk from the standard Stockport price of 5d (£1.45) per quart to 3.5d (87p) per quart. Most farmers, however, wanted yet further rises in the price of milk or they threatened to send their spare milk to cheese factories where it would give them a much greater return of profits.

The demand for electricity was rising and the supplies of coal were decreasing as yet more miners enlisted. Coal was needed for gas lighting, but more supplies of coal were being demanded by the navy and manufacturers. As the autumn wore on there were many complaints about the lighting restrictions and darkened streets. With the restrictions on shop opening times, the smaller traders were hurt more because 75% of their business came from supplying 'odds and ends' after the bigger stores had closed. The only exceptions to these reduced hours were for medicines, newspapers, the sale of cooked food to take away, and for hairdressers or barbers to attend to 'after work customers'.

However, while the population was 'all in this together' and everyone was supposed to be suffering from shortages and restrictions in equal measure, the *Stockport Advertiser* ran several fashion features and advertisements for silks, satins, furs, and at Hallowe'en it was announced that there would be a revival of the evening dress for the coming winter. 'Demand,' said the paper, 'has been shown in more exclusive houses for lovely evening gowns.' Cotton workers, sitting in their cramped kitchens, unable to afford more than one gill of milk a day, must have read that news in disbelief when the same newspaper was full of pleas for thrift and economy and the stopping of wasteful habits. Even Lloyd George and Bonar Law renounced their parliamentary salaries for the duration of the war.

At the other end of the scale a clog fund for poor children in Stockport had just been started and Stockport suffragettes were personally funding beds in a Corsican hospital for Serbian refugees. Stockport Infirmary was also making fresh pleas for support and funding, citing rising food and commodity prices and staff wages. The hospital's expenditure throughout 1915 had been £26 (£1820) per week more than its income and there was now a serious deficit.

Stockport had not fared well either in establishing national war savings associations. Ideally, each workplace should have had one, yet there were only nine in Stockport compared to other towns, some less

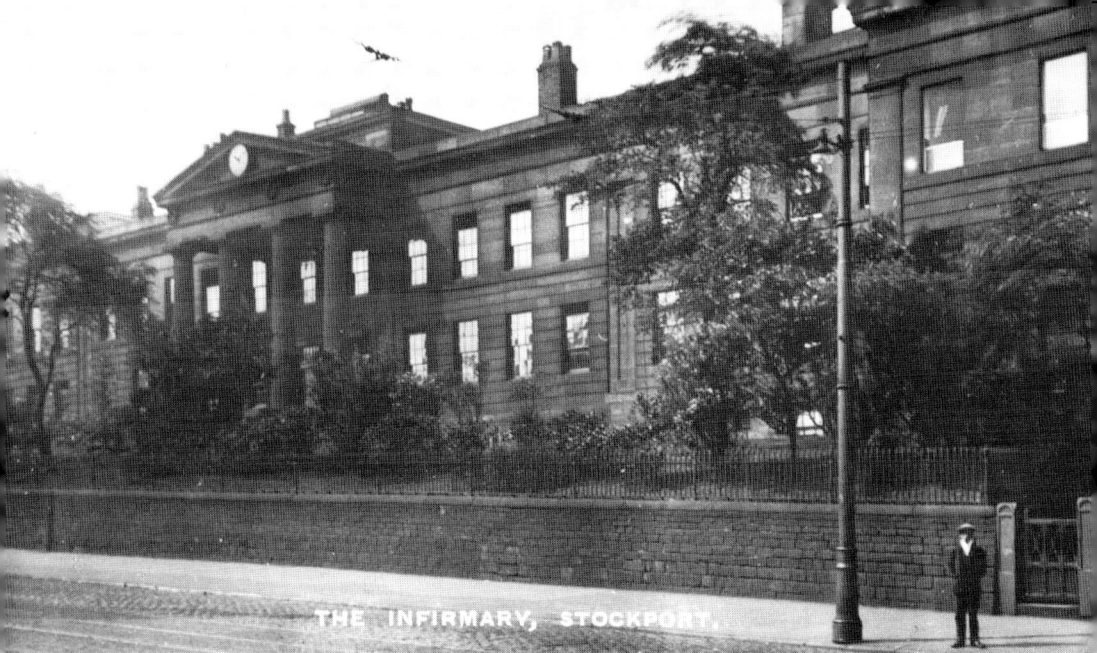

Stockport Infirmary as a military hospital c1916

than half the size of Stockport, yet some of which had as many as sixty such associations.

Christmas was approaching and in Stockport a sixpenny fund was started to provide Christmas comforts for wounded soldiers. Collecting boxes for sixpenny (£1.75) pieces were placed in shops and newsagents. The reduced opening hours for shops were suspended for two weeks before Christmas, but Christmas shopping was condemned as selfish and indulgent. All efforts and spare cash, it was said, should be directed towards soldiers, sailors and the production of munitions.

Despite the advertisements for Christmas gifts and fashions in the paper, there were numerous ideas put forward in the *Stockport Advertiser* for saving yet more money. One lady wrote a letter describing French frugality as the model to adopt. Other suggestions included taxing restaurants and afternoon tea, forbidding the making of cakes, abandoning motor drives for pleasure, and spending absolutely no money on fashion. This did not stop the newspaper from running an editorial feature on 'Christmas shopping and attractive displays in Stockport'.

Food supplies had also become a worry and farmers were being asked to each grow at least 100 acres of wheat and 3 acres of potatoes in 1917. Christmas cakes and puddings were made with less fruit, butter and sugar, fresh fruit was scarce, and cooking in hay-boxes was advocated. Using this method, food was brought to boiling point and then insulated in the box so that the items would cook in the heat held by the insulation. It worked well although food took a long time to cook.

In the event, the third Christmas of the war turned out to be 'sober, thoughtful and subdued'. There was snow and the tramway service found itself dislocated in dense fog. Rail services were reduced and fares were increased to discourage travel, and soldiers were forbidden to travel on trains 22 – 25 December. The Christmas pantomime at the Stockport Theatre Royal this year was *Aladdin*, and many must have wished for their own personal genie who would provide as much heat and food and light as they could wish for, but most of all who would stop the fighting and bring their loved ones safely home.

CHAPTER 4

1917

❖

The year began with the ubiquitous list of casualties – yet more names to add to the roll of honour and more heartbreak for some families. Local hospitals struggled to cope with the numbers of wounded and gassed soldiers coming to the town for treatment and convalescence. Prices of food and fuel continued to rise steadily and there were worries about restricted supplies, especially of wheat and sugar. The government suspended the credit system in shops to try and enforce economy. While this move curbed extravagance and increased cash flow, it made life difficult for those paid monthly or quarterly salaries. It also made life harder for many tradesmen who made credit arrangements between themselves, allowing bulk buying of items that could then be sold on to retail outlets.

Shortage of labour in Stockport Gasworks meant that any street lighting improvements were slow to materialise. Local train services were greatly reduced, especially those through Edgeley and Tiviot Dale. Fares were also increased by 50% due to shortages of fuel and labour (117,000 of the total 600,000 railway workers had enlisted) and the fact that a growing number of trains were being sent to the continent for war service. A strike by Stockport Tramways workers over wages, advances, and alterations to working conditions was quickly settled because transport was essential for the workers.

The effects of the short- or double-shift system in Stockport schools was becoming apparent. There was a reduction of syllabuses, courses

Stockport Technical School c1908

were shortened, and subject matter treated in less depth. Time needed for revision was lost and there was a marked decline in accuracy and the finishing of work, although there did not seem to be any decline in the children's abilities. However, it was decided that the general school system should be reformed. The school leaving age was to be raised, there was to be compulsory attendance at secondary school, and facilities provided for more children to enjoy a secondary and perhaps even university education, as well as courses at the technical schools. Teachers' claims for salary increases were ignored, although traditionally their pay was quite low, and there were rumours that soon no one would want to teach, not even girls. The women's columns of the newspaper were full of news of fashion, materials and sewing, not so much making garments for the troops but to keep up with latest 'must-have' dresses, skirts and tops. Frock coats seemed to be all the rage for women, but they did at least serve a kind of dual purpose.

At the same time strenuous efforts were being made to publicise and promote the war loan scheme to all classes of the community, especially by Stockport Savings Bank, because Stockport was not meeting the war loan targets the town had been set in accordance with the size of its population. It was emphasised that all mills, workshops, firms and companies should do their bit collectively as well as individuals.

In mid-January, the *Advertiser* printed an obituary for John Froggat of Offerton. He had worked in a brass foundry and then as a plumber and a gas fitter before enjoying a sprightly old age and dying at 102. What was remarkable about him were the changes that had taken place within his lifetime. He was born in 1814, the year before Waterloo, into a largely rural Britain. He saw six monarchs sit on the throne of England: George III; George IV; William IV; Victoria; Edward VII; and George V. And he remembered seeing ox roasts in Stockport market square for the coronations of George IV and William IV. He was eleven when the first railway, between Stockton and Darlington, opened, and he lived to see the aftermath of Napoleon's defeat and his subsequent exile to St Helena as well as the full impact of the industrial revolution and cottonopolis, the building of the empire, the American Civil War, the Crimean War, the Boer War and the first two years of the First World War. He also witnessed the development of motor cars, 'lurries', aeroplanes and tanks, advances in medicine and the use of anaesthetics, as well as the advent of the telephone, radio communications and moving pictures. Mr Froggatt took a keen interest in the war and followed its progress closely until he died. Sadly, his thoughts and comments have not survived but he saw hostilities reach a point where the merchant navy was much depleted, not to say almost destroyed, and the prospect of the country being saddled with a national debt of £5,000,000,000 (£350,000,000,000) as a result of the war.

Stockport Corporation began assessing land available for cultivation and had powers to insist it should be used for food production. Corporation departments who owned land began growing potatoes, and the Smallholdings and Allotment Committee rented out allotments of

Buxton Road, Stockport c1913

some 300-400 yards in size at 5/- (about £18) per annum per plot. Local private landowners refused to give any land at all for allotments, however, but the government passed the Cultivation of Land Order, which enabled the Smallholdings and Allotments Committee to take whatever land was wanted or needed for allotments. Land in Great Moor, Reddish and Heaton Norris was selected and, in addition, the site of the Great Moor junior school bordering Westland Road and Southwood Road, plus a field on Buxton Road opposite the Crown Inn, as well as land in Heaton Norris adjoining Thornfield Road recreation ground.

Cultivation of public parks was under discussion. Folk were encouraged to grow potatoes and seed potatoes were to be supplied at a reasonable price. Those in the more outlying country districts were asked to keep a pig as well. Cheshire farmers, still persisting in their demands for skilled agricultural workers to be recalled from the Front, voiced fears that producing supplementary foodstuffs in this way from parks and allotments would force down prices, but no one was listening. Food was expensive and shortages were occurring. People were frightened and in some cases hungry. If folk could grow their own and thereby gain extra food to feed themselves and their families, they were not going to be concerned with the cash flow problems of local farmers. Officialdom simply took the view that it was now 'all hands to the plough', but it was agreed that a number of soldiers from the Home Defence units could be switched to agricultural work.

The Ministry of Agriculture expressed the intention to train an army of women to work on the land as well as insisting that city dwellers should also join in growing potatoes so that farmers could concentrate on growing corn. Corn, potatoes and pigs became known as 'the big three'. The prices of oats, wheat and potatoes had been fixed, so there was now no opportunity for profiteering. The *Stockport Advertiser* began a weekly column of hints for allotment holders advising on a number of matters, such as what vegetables to grow and when to plant them, how to deal with seed potatoes, artificial manure, and the benefits of small 'sets'.

As Lloyd George had said, the war was about money as much as, if not more than, anything else and it was costing the country £42,000,000 (£2,054,000,000) per year. Only £10,000,000 (just under £489,000,000) was being raised through taxation so there was a huge shortfall. Initially, applications in multiples of £5 (about £245) were requested for the war loan and it was again emphasised that every mill, workshop and company should contribute. Later loan applications would be extended to all individuals for any amount up £5, which they would be allowed to pay for in instalments by buying special stamps and sticking them on a war loans card. Ever since he had discovered, in 1915, that the nation was spending more on drink than on munitions, Lloyd George was determined that the whole country should accept it had to pay for the war somehow and that everyone should play a part, however great or small. Economy and efficiency were, he said, more important than ever. Self-denial and restrictions on purchases must be practised.

MPs followed the example of Lloyd George and Bonar Law in not drawing their parliamentary salaries for the duration of the war to demonstrate that everyone was in it together, whatever their standing, status or job, and even the king announced that the royal family were living on war bread, porridge and bloaters (a type of fish). George V was acutely aware that his whole family was German in origin and he was therefore anxious to show complete solidarity with the British people. In July he changed his family name of Saxe-Coburg-Gotha to that of Windsor.

Voluntary fundraising for the troops was going well. A cheque for £1,800 (£88,000) was presented to the Heaton Chapel, Heaton Moor and Heaton Mersey Fund for totally disabled soldiers' and sailors' homes. Regular flag days raised hundreds (thousands) of pounds for comforts for the troops, Belgian refugees, the Red Cross, wounded soldiers and military hospitals. Food parcels were sent to prisoners-of-war twice a month and could contain 10lb (just under 5kg) of food. Typical rations would include:

- 1 tin of beef stew
- 2 tins of potted meat

- 1 tin of bloater (fish) paste
- 1 tin of sausages
- 1 tin of pineapple
- 1 tin of peas
- 1 packet of soup cubes
- 1 packet of grape nuts (cereal made from wheat and barley)
- ½lb (250g) of sugar
- ¼lb (125g) of tea

There were between 100 and 150 men from Stockport receiving these parcels by 1917. In addition, once a month, a small parcel containing soap, candles, cigarettes or tobacco, would be sent to each man. Three hundred ladies from Stockport were also making clothes or comforts and collecting fresh eggs for the wounded and those in nursing homes. Unfortunately, not everyone in the Stockport area heeded the pleas for self-sacrifice and many either couldn't or wouldn't economise on food. There seemed to be a 'well, if I don't he or she will' mindset when it came to buying or hoarding food. In vain, the local paper and the mayor issued appeals for voluntary personal rationing of potatoes and sugar, and a 10% reduction in meat consumption. It was also suggested that better-off folk should buy the dearer cuts of meat so that the cheaper cuts were left for those who were struggling to make ends meet. All this fell on deaf ears, which resulted in a shortage of potatoes in Stockport shops and on the local markets, so potatoes were then rationed to 1lb (500g) per person per week. This worked out at about three good medium sized potatoes for everyone, but as the poor relied on potatoes it was a terrible hardship for many.

In Stockport 'potato hogs' went round the allotments digging up and stealing potatoes, despite a penalty of six months imprisonment if caught. The local newspaper slammed 'careless selfish hoarders' especially when bread and flour were also rationed. Lord Devonport condemned those hoarding tea, coffee, cocoa and flour as 'contemptible'. Hoarding was a national problem, as well as local to Stockport, and consequently, on 5 April, the Food Hoarding Order came into force, making it illegal to buy large amounts of foodstuffs and threatening penalties to those hoarding foodstuffs in short supply. The importance of allotment production was becoming paramount and each week the *Stockport Advertiser* suggested types of vegetable to plant and offered hints on keeping poultry. Sparrows and rats were proving a local nuisance by attacking crops on allotments, so clubs were formed and members were paid to kill these pests. The going rate was 1/- (about £2.50) for a dozen rat's tails and from 3d (63p) to 1d (21p) per dozen sparrows, depending on their size. The cull of sparrows proved problematical because it was the house sparrows that were causing the nuisance but many people were unable to tell the difference between the house sparrow and its cousin the hedge sparrow. Hedge sparrows were beneficial and necessary to the ecological process and real damage was done as a result.

There was a national war on wastage and a food economy campaign began in Stockport. The country's food stocks were now seriously low and meatless days were instigated at restaurants and hotels on Wednesdays and Fridays. Co-operative kitchens were advocated, and one of the first was the YMCA war workers restaurant in Stockport, which proved to be very successful. No meal cost more than 1s 3d (around £3) and they were nourishing as well as cheap. Some sixty to seventy workers were employed and some days as many as 1,800 meals were served. A rigid food economy was required and all children were made to eat crusts of bread and deaf ears were turned to protests. There were shortages and hardships everywhere, but country folk were generally a little better fed than townspeople, while the very rich took to buying smuggled food.

Despite everything, food and fuel prices continued to rise steadily, which caused problems for many working folk in the town. There was a loss on the gas undertaking of the council and the price of gas for street lamps went up. Tram fares rose. This was followed by a rates increase of 3d (63p) in the pound (then 240 pence). Stockport council had wanted a 6d increase because a 3d increase was insufficient to pay increased wages and bonuses. Education was deemed 'a big drain' but still received more funding while funding for health, highways, parks and the sewage department was cut. There were fears for the survival

Stockport Sunday School c1912

of the Stockport hatting trade because import restrictions had been placed on skins, furs, silk and platting, so that raw supplies were limited. The cotton trade was also facing problems from a shortage of raw supplies and from cotton duty tariffs imposed by India. Despite this, cotton operatives had gone on strike for a 10% wage rise and had received it. Reddish cotton spinners wanted to employ young teenagers (aged 13 – 14 years) as their wage costs were lower. Several mills had gone over to munitions work while Joseph Dunkerley & Son set up a munitions works in Stockport Sunday School and advertised for hundreds of workers. Local teachers, however, refused an annual war bonus and held out for the long promised good regular wage increments, but turned down a flat-rate advance of £10 – £15 per annum because this would cause the rates to rise even more sharply.

A national volunteers' service was organised so that men who could not serve in the forces could be formed into bands of itinerant workers who would go where the need was. Initially, under this system men were told they would need to join a relevant trade union and receive a trade card, which would then allow them to be accepted for the work.

Land Army girls with Shire horses in Bramhall 1916 (courtesy of Stockport Local Studies)

However, widespread abuse led to the trade card system being scrapped and certificates issued instead to justify the wearing of war work service badges. Half-a-million men were required in the agriculture, woodlands, shipbuilding, construction and engineering industries. Although there were around 250,000 women already working as farm labourers in various parts of the country, the government now set up the Women's Land Army and advertised for the recruitment of women from towns and cities to grow and harvest 'victory crops' and to help with other aspects of farm work. Ten thousand were wanted, plus 5,000 milkers, 4,000 fieldworkers and 1,000 carters. The benefits offered were generous:

- free uniform
- maintenance during training and periods of unemployment
- travelling expenses to work
- 18/- (about £45) per week in wages
- inspected and approved housing accommodation
- work on selected farms
- promotion for good work
- post-war special facilities for settlement at home or abroad

Women flocked to volunteer and proved to be enthusiastic and adaptable workers. Stockport volunteers were sent to train at Holmes Chapel in Cheshire and Cheshire farmers now found they had no choice but to accept female labour. Stockport Theatre Royal, which seemed to have a talent for irony, now chose to play Harold Brighouse's Lancashire comedy *Hobson's Choice*.

Although Easter was quite late this year (it fell in mid-April), the weather was cold and there were still vestiges of frost and even snow. Folks shivered and tried not to use up their fuel stocks, although Easter Sunday and Monday had really bad weather. It just added to the general gloom and depression from which the country was now suffering as the war dragged on with no end in sight. If there was an upside it was that the war had reduced pauperism because of the need for fighting men and the shortage of male labour. Men from the workhouses and even tramps were either joining up or finding gainful employment. However, there was now a recruiting campaign for men up to 50 years of age. It was a desperate measure and although there were 2,000,000 men in that age group within the country it was acknowledged that many might not be fit to fight.

Meanwhile, the fashion columns of the *Stockport Advertiser* were determined to remain upbeat and reported excitedly that the frock coat was finally to be replaced in the summer by the jumper blouse, but this news seemed to be greeted with muted enthusiasm. As the fuel shortages worsened, however, the *Advertiser* recommended its female readers to 'take a leaf out of their Eastern sisters' cookery books', and either cook single pot meals or to place a hot-plate over a single gas ring so that several cooking pots could be accommodated at once.

Stockport stepped up its food economy campaign 'waste not, want not', making appeals in the newspapers, theatres and cinemas, while the mayor spoke of 'the duty of housewives' and made a plea for folk to eat 1lb (about 550g) less bread each week because, otherwise, the country's wheat supplies might run out six weeks before the harvest. Stockport food campaign held a traders' week to persuade people of the urgent need for frugality, economy and sharing as well as the necessity for voluntary rationing. But, although food shortages and restrictions were becoming serious problems, they were often evaded by the better-off folk, especially in the case of sugar. There was little sugar available now and it was often only sold with a minimum purchase of other groceries. Sugar lumps were greatly favoured over granulated or loaf sugar. So far there had been no enforcement by the government of sugar sales restrictions and many people now wanted compulsory rationing of sugar so that everyone got a little. Bread was another matter. Loaves had to weigh at least 1lb (about 550g) or an even number of pounds in weight, and only certain loaf styles were permitted.

Although the British Red Cross society in Heaton Chapel had taken over the Reform Clubhouse in Heaton Moor as a hospital, Stockport Infirmary still needed money to complete its extension for 170 patients. The demand for beds for military patients was rapidly exceeding the supply so Stepping Hill was now required as a military hospital. This necessitated moving all its union patients to Shaw Heath hospital. Stockport open air music festival, which included the choruses from the *Messiah*, was to be held in Vernon Park and the funds raised given to the Infirmary. It was hoped that this might ease the shortage of beds for military patients. More women were desperately needed as nurses and the Women's Land Army also wanted more volunteers. Industries in the town needed workers as well, but there were many problems.

Although the mills and workshops had closed from Thursday – Tuesday over Easter, the holiday had been so poor that they proposed to close for a week at Whitsun (in addition to the wakes week in

Vernon Park, Stockport c1909

August), although in the event only Thursday afternoon – Tuesday morning was taken off work. There were no excursions and few travel facilities available. Munitions workers could not take holidays and did not think mill workers should either. The engineers were undecided.

There was a good deal of worker discontent, especially among engineers. The Bleachers' Association was in difficulty and suffering a shortage of raw materials. War bonuses were a big question and were proving a problem for the council who couldn't afford to pay them. Corporation employees and tradesmen wanted bonuses paid in accordance with TUC guidelines. Local teachers refused war bonuses, but wanted larger salaries to meet the high prices of food and fuel. Gas workers were still hankering after war bonuses, but the council were more interested in the future of the electricity supplies, having invested in state-of-the-art equipment. There was also a strike by stokers at the gasworks over an arbitrator's award and disputes over the length of the working week. This resulted in much irritation and inconvenience and everyone felt that the gasworkers were holding Stockport to ransom. Great prejudice and hostility was shown to female tram conductresses by their male counterparts when the women went on strike because, unlike the men, they had not been paid any war bonus for the same work. The local paper, ever conservative in tone and attitude, wrote a sarcastic piece about the strike headed 'serious trousers versus frivolous petticoats'. To the men at the Front who read the *Stockport Advertiser* sent out to them by friends and relatives, all the strikes were incomprehensible, counter-productive and unpatriotic.

Each week the newspaper ran a 'war pensions and help column' for the dependants of soldiers and sailors who found themselves in difficulties. A recent pensions' tribunal had also discovered that both soldiers and sailors were dissatisfied with pensions awarded and, although officers' pensions were to be re-assessed, it was only for those in the army and not for those serving in the navy. During this grim time, with all the discontent, shortages and talk of economies, Stockport co-operative society decided to 'lighten up' by holding a sale of 'forty ladies black silk and satin coats' at 25/- (about £61) each.

The summer was making up for the poor performance of the weather earlier in the year and prospects for the harvest looked good. The *Stockport Advertiser* allowed itself to wax lyrical and wrote 'hay cutting will be good and there are exquisitely fragranced wild roses and honeysuckle in bloom in the hedgerows'. However, the paper added, the corncrakes were having a bad time of it as 'the grass cutters drove them from meadow to meadow'. Life was about to get even worse for the unfortunate corncrakes as some '60,000 acres of grassland in Cheshire were to be broken to grow wheat'. Nationally, this translated into restoring the cultivation of 3,000,000 acres, which had been allowed to lapse over the previous forty years, and this was authorised by the passing of the Corn Production Act in the summer of 1917.

Despite the problems of the corncrake the harvest proved to be a good one for wheat, barley, oats, potatoes, mangoes, peas and beans but only average for the fruits such as apples, pears, plums, cherries and hops. Female harvest workers also thoroughly proved themselves to the incredulous amazement of all Cheshire farmers.

Lord Rhondda prohibited the buying and selling of wheat, barley, oats, rye and the main crops of potatoes except under the auspices of a nationally appointed food controller. There was to be 'state milling' of all British and foreign grains and granaries built for storage. Flour and bread prices were to be fixed weekly and would be the same all over the country, and this was intended to eradicate profiteering. Stockport allotment holders had produced surplus food but this was easily disposed of to family and friends, and the other townspeople. The local allotments committee turned a blind eye and did nothing official about it. Besides, they were engaged in trying to resolve the question of whether marrows were fruits and dealing with a plague of mosquitos, who were proving to be real pests on the allotments.

Despite the successful harvest, minimum agricultural wages around the country were reduced from 30/- (around £73) a week to 25/- (about £61), because the farmers could not afford it and it was stated that agricultural wages simply could not be as high as industrial wages. The lower amount was supposed to be 'with all found', but in practice this generally did not happen.

The big subject of debate in the summer of 1917, besides the war, was the Electoral Reform Bill. The main changes were two-fold. Electoral boundaries were to be re-drawn, 'rotten boroughs' were to be abolished and some seats redistributed to industrial towns. A rotten borough was a town or village that had parliamentary representation but few, if any, voters. The best known example is that of Old Sarum, which returned two members to parliament but had no population. Under the parliamentary divisions Cheshire was to have nine county and five borough members, making a total of fourteen members. The county boroughs would return as follows:

- Stockport two members
- Birkenhead two members
- Wallasey one member

Stockport's electoral boundaries were also extended to include Reddish and Heaton Norris voters. There were no real objections to the electoral changes within the town, but there were many objections from Cheshire to changes within the county. Elections were also to be held on a single day and not over three weeks, as had been the custom previously.

The other major and hotly debated change was that women over 30 were to be given the vote, although there were some restrictions that would not be removed for another decade. The suffragettes, of whom there had been a large and active group in Stockport, had been campaigning for women to have the vote for several years before the war but had put their campaign on hold after hostilities commenced to help with the war effort. The government had to admit that women had proved wonderfully supportive and adaptive during the war and deserved the right to vote. The act was introduced by the Home Secretary, George Cave, with the words:

> *War by all classes of our countrymen has brought us nearer together, has opened men's eyes, and removed misunderstandings on all sides. It has made it, I think, impossible that ever again, at all events in the lifetime of the present generation, there should be a revival of the old class feeling which was responsible for so much, and among other things, for the exclusion for a period, of so many of our population from the class of electors. I think I need say no more to justify the extension of this franchise.*

There was almost total cross party assent for the bill in the House of Commons, but there was opposition from the House of Lords. However, Lord Curzon, president of the National League for Opposing Woman Suffrage, did not want to clash with the Commons so did not oppose the bill in the Lords. Without his support, most of the other opponents lost heart and the bill was successfully passed through both houses. It was a major tribute to the role played by women in the war and paved the way for women to train and practise as doctors, dentists,

George Wardle, MP for Stockport c1915

lawyers, solicitors and police women. Some were even considered to serve as justices of the peace. Encouraged by this acknowledgement of the roles women could now play in society, the local WEA recommended that the municipal scholarship scheme should now be extended to include girls at Stockport Grammar School and Stockport Girls High School.

In late July, arrangements were made by representatives of the French Socialist Party, the British Labour Party and the Russians for the second inter-allied socialist conference, which would be held in London in August. Ramsay McDonald led a small expedition to Paris for talks to organise the conference. The general aims were victory in Europe and, after the peace, the restoration of Belgium plus an end to secret diplomacy and the interest of arms makers. One member of his party was Mr George Wardle, Labour MP for Stockport. The *Stockport Advertiser* was incandescent with rage when this fact was discovered. It had always been reserved and cautious about the Labour movement, frequently suspecting ulterior motives where there were none, and criticising the party whenever it got the chance. Now the paper launched itself into a furious tirade against the Labour Party in general and Mr Wardle in particular, demanding that he explain himself to the town. Mr Wardle saw no particular need to explain anything. The matter was clear enough. So he ignored the paper, which continued to rage against him for several months.

Part of the problem was that the *Advertiser* was very hostile to pacifists and conscientious objectors and the paper assumed they were all socialists. Many were, in fact, Quakers or Jehovah's Witnesses and it was an over-simplification to identify all members of any creed as having exactly the same beliefs.

By the end of August, introduction of the first official rationing of foodstuffs began. The food control committee in Stockport, having spent some considerable time organising its membership, which had to include at least one female and at least one Labour member, issued sugar rationing tickets. Sugar registration cards were to be distributed by the post office in early September. Retailers were to ensure that no customer was supplied with sugar twice in one week. Caterers were to be allowed for weekly vouchers for their sugar allowances. The sugar rationing scheme would not be in full operation until January in 1918. Meat and bread were to be rationed shortly. Profiteers and the public had been unable or unwilling to regulate themselves on a voluntary basis, so there was now a basic food policy for rationing coming into operation. It had three basic aims:

- food supplies were to be conserved
- food supplies were to be shared equally between rich and poor
- food prices were to be kept down

It was also likely that coal would be rationed as well. To control coal rations, depots for storage were set-up in Town Yard, the old gasworks yard, Heaton Lane and Reddish. A retail prices coal order was passed to regulate prices so that everyone would be able to afford some coal. It was now already 7s 6d (about £18.50) per ton dearer than at the start of the war. Coal supplies were also being sent to the continent for the war effort and stocks at home were dwindling rapidly, as there were fewer miners than ever before. The food control committee would be responsible for administering coal rationing. A Meat (Maximum Price) Order had also been passed and butchers had to 'post in a conspicuous position' a complete price list of all the cuts of meat sold by their shop.

One of the biggest conflicts, however, was between the food control committee and the retailers over milk prices. The food control committee fixed milk prices at 5d (about £1) per quart (just under a litre) but the retailers were selling the milk at 6d (£1.20) to 7d (£1.40) a quart. This was, of course, all due to making profits. The food control committee then decided to sell directly to the retailers in order to cut out the middlemen, and a price of 6d a quart was finally agreed. It was a necessary measure. Milk was an essential part of everyone's diet, especially children, and prices had risen 100% since 1914. Lord Rhondda, who oversaw food rationing projects at national level, was concerned that 'the harvests of the world cannot meet ours and our allies' needs in the next twelve months' unless 'rigid economy was voluntarily effected' or there would need to be a 'compulsory system of rationing'. He utterly condemned the problems caused by 'the malignity of a few' and 'the folly and heedlessness of many'.

Stockport life, however, continued to be like a 'tale of two cities'. It was noted in the local paper that the war had wrought changes in ballroom dancing so that 'partners no longer held each other lightly by the waist and hand for neither was dependent on the other'. This revolution in dancing had apparently been caused by enthusiasm for the tango. There were parallel columns of newsprint devoted to beaver being in vogue for the autumn fashions, the lovely colours of velvet available, and that Paris dressmakers were having to reduce woollen material for women's dresses from 6 yards (5.5m) to 4½ yards (4.1m) alongside the problems of food and fuel shortages, and spade-workers' hints on growing haricot beans, beetroot, celery and 'useful leeks'. Yet the war loan and war bond schemes in the town were under-supported and consistently failed to meet government targets, and it was disconcerting that none of the local private landowners would give land for cultivation of food until compelled to do so by government sanction.

Food queues remained a problem and so did folk buying more than their fair share and hoarding supplies. There were regular outbursts and sideswipes by members of the Conservative and Liberal parties at the fledgling Independent Labour Party, and the minority parties representing discharged heroes who feared that the 'land fit for heroes' promised for returning soldiers and sailors after the war would turn out to be a total myth.

In December, the Liberals and Independents secured control of some of Stockport Town Council's most important committees (which included the watch, gas, health and finance committees) by, according to the Conservatives, 'methods worthy of the Bolsheviks!' There had been no committee lists exchanged and no arrangements made between the parties, which was apparently the 'time-honoured practice'. The Liberals and Independents 'went in determined to upset the apple-cart'. Conservatives, who were 'naturally loyal and faithful' had been badly betrayed. Heaton Norris in particular, which had Independent members on the council, was verbally attacked for not understanding this basic principle. The 'old order' was proving anxious to hold on to power, perhaps not realising that the war had changed the former way of life forever. It made a sad contrast to many other north-western towns, who appeared to be more prepared to set aside personal, political and financial differences in order to defeat the kaiser.

At the end of November, a Reddish man, Sergeant Joseph Lister of the Lancashire Fusiliers, became the first Stockport man to win the Victoria Cross. It was awarded for his bravery and military ability in capturing 100 German soldiers and was a badly needed item of cheer for the town, which was not looking forward to Christmas.

The fourth Christmas of the war proved to be a gloomy and subdued affair. Cakes and puddings were severely limited in size and content due to food shortages and rationing of sugar, dried fruits, butter, eggs and flour. Puff pastry was absolutely forbidden and other pastry was scarce. For those who could afford a chicken or turkey, accompaniments were mashed potato or boiled rice with dripping, onions and herbs. Cold dishes included sheep's head or pickled tongue. Rice cake, made from rice-flour, sugar, margarine, one egg and a little lemon, was a treat.

There were no trams or newspapers on Christmas Day. Shoppers were told to carry their own parcels weighing under 7lb (just over 3kg) and to bring their own paper and string to package their purchases. On a positive note, the Primrose League were busy promoting a toy-making industry in England, despite the government commandeering empty or available factories for war work. Toy-making in the UK had

Ward 2, Heaton Mersey Red Cross Hospital c1915 (courtesy of Stockport Local Studies)

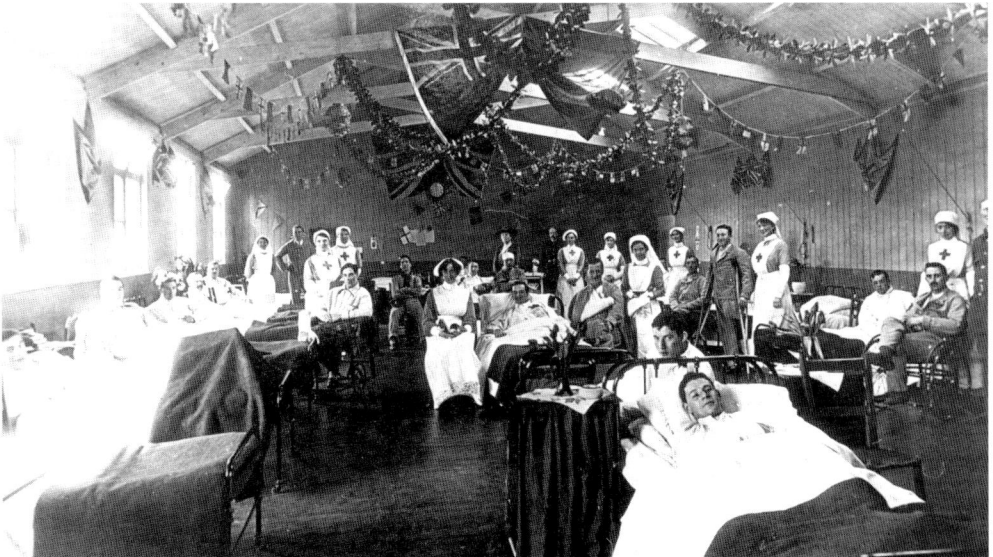

suffered as a result of the war and Japanese toys had replaced the German and Austrian toys popular before the war.

The Minnehaha Minstrels gave a successful concert in Stockport and organised an auction, both to raise much needed funds to keep prisoners-of-war from the town supplied with food parcels and comforts. There were a number of appeals for Christmas festivities and treats for the wounded in Stockport's military hospitals and institutions, which now included

- Stockport Infirmary
- Reddish Military Hospital
- Dialstone Lane Hospital
- Sir Ralph Pendlebury Auxiliary Home Hospital
- Stepping Hill Hospital
- Workhouse
- Offerton Industrial School
- Stockport Girls Industrial School
- Bishop Brown's Memorial Industrial School

The *Stockport Advertiser* published a memorial card for the relatives of fallen soldiers and sailors and devoted a three-column spread to the Christmas message from the Right Reverend Bishop Welldon, Dean of Manchester, headed 'Peace among the Nations'. He asked if Christmas was a failure but rejected this notion on the grounds that children were 'pure and innocent like the Divine Child'. He thought of Christmas as a 'reconciler of old memories and old joys and peace among men'. Asserting that 'democracy makes for peace', he saw 'a war such as this a bitter satire upon civilization and Christianity', and preached his own desperate message of hope that the war really would soon be over.

The Theatre Royal, again appropriately enough, had chosen *Beauty and the Beast* as their Christmas pantomime. The children probably enjoyed Christmas rather more than their parents, who looked ahead to a new year filled with food shortages, a lack of fuel, more economies and restrictions, and further appeals for their hard-earned cash to finance the seemingly never-ending hostilities.

CHAPTER 5

1918

The year began with a lantern lecture by Stockport War Savings Committee on war in the air and the story of Britain's supposed air supremacy. It was the first time that air warfare had been used and the development of fighter planes was still in its infancy. One British general even said that 'the airplane is useless for the purposes of war'. The German Fokker triplane was the most advanced aircraft of the time, but in England the Avro K and the Sopwith Camel gained good reputations as fighter planes, although they look like clumsy toys compared to the sleek, sophisticated and highly technical Black Hawk jets that now help to protect British airspace. Flying increased the necessity for warm clothing and the Italians invented clothing heated by a storage battery to counteract the intense cold of high altitude flying.

Early in 1918, Lieutenant A. H. Butterworth of Stockport was awarded the military cross for 'bringing down two Bosche machines in air fighting'. At this time, Stockport was only meeting about a sixth of its allocated war bonds quota necessary for financing all aspects of the war and the town was being strongly urged to 'do its share'. Most people's interests, however, were more down to earth and centred on food and fuel shortages.

Butchers were no longer able to source meat to sell at controlled prices. One of the problems was that consumers did not want meat with bone but the butchers were forced to buy the lot, bones and all. The government requisitioned the supplies of Australian and New Zealand meat, which had managed to reach British shores as well as much of the Irish meat. Most butchers were therefore solely reliant on local home grown meat. Chickens reared by farmers or on allotments were a supplement but utility here was also advocated. Consequently, while the Sussex and Rhode Island Reds were popular breeds, Cochins, Silkies and Bantams were not wanted.

Distribution of meat, butter, margarine, tea, bacon and sugar was also causing severe problems due to reductions in transport and the numbers of shop assistants available to serve customers. Milk distribution was a major problem. Children under 5 were supposed to have at least one pint daily, but the dispute over costs of production and profits from sales still raged. Local farmers refused to supply any milk in Romiley, forcing residents to seize milk from neighbouring areas. Some farmers withheld milk for cheese or butter making, although others would unofficially supply milk to residents who fetched it themselves. There was condemnation on both sides while some babies and children went short of milk. Finally, the local food controller was given powers to requisition all milk supplies and milk distribution was then operated on a fair basis.

To make matters worse, there was a potato blight threatening all crops while 'daddy longlegs' and 'wireworms' were posing a nuisance to allotments. Communal kitchens were being proposed, to save on fuel and bulk buy foodstuffs. There should be 'one in each considerable street'. It was also proposed that there should be communal laundries, which would save on the construction of individual wash houses for each property, and communal nurseries, all of which would be commercially self-supporting. However, staff would be needed and it was lamented that domestic economy was now the 'Cinderella of professions', with a steep decline in the number of students as a result of the war, and also girls could find better paid jobs. They were now training for jobs in police work or as Marconi mechanics, while skilled female hairdressers were much in demand, and the munitions factories still paid high wages.

Gas supplies to mills, hat-works, laundries and public buildings were cut because a shortage of labour meant delays in processing the gas and there had been extra demand due to the cold weather. Coal was becoming quite scarce as well due to the reduction in the number of miners and also because quantities were requisitioned by the government to be sent to the Front.

Meanwhile, the Liberals and Independents were experiencing great difficulty in controlling the council. The Conservatives, feeling that the 'war truce had been dishonoured' by the loss of their control of some committees, would not co-operate. They called for committee restructuring and then refused to negotiate or compromise. As a result of this in-fighting, the town council found it had virtually no minutes at its next meeting. The only exceptions were those from the Heaton Norris Committee and from a special war bonus sub-committee. The rest of the committees were in 'a state of suspended animation' with the Liberals displaying 'no repentance for this state of affairs'.

Meanwhile, the Registrar of Friendly Societies refused to affiliate a Co-operative Society to the Labour Party. There was still much anti-socialist feeling, a 'common enemy', opposition to which might have united the Conservatives, Liberals and Independents. However, there was also anger among the political parties over proposed trade with Germany after the war and the suggestion that British-made machinery should be sold and installed in that country.

While the council was engaged by its disunity, Coronation Mills in South Reddish made what, to them, was a startling discovery. The owners had decided that a working week of $55\frac{1}{2}$ hours was too long, especially for women and girls. Working hours were therefore reduced to forty-nine hours per week: 8am – 6pm Monday – Friday (which included an hour for dinner) and 8am – noon on Saturdays. They found that the workers were brighter and more alert and that, amazingly, output did not suffer. Consequently, there was no reduction in wages. It was a win-win situation. Most mills were restricted to 60% production at this point, but their profits were good, and 10% dividends were the rule, despite the difficulties the cotton trade faced.

The council finally resolved the deadlock over their committees but

Female workers drilling tank engine cylinders at Mirrlees c1918 (courtesy of Stockport Local Studies)

the Conservatives remained deeply unhappy that the Liberals had 'broken the Party pledge'. The war bonds submissions were now only 1/15 of the quota set for the town (according to its population) by the government. The mayor, anxious to reverse this state of affairs and to draw attention away from the troubled workings of the council, blamed the lack of interest on the fact that Stockport had no tank to stimulate interest in supporting the war effort. Tank parts were actually manufactured in the town, but a previous request for a tank had been declined as many local companies had already put money into funding a Manchester tank. Finally, it was agreed that a tank should be sent to Stockport to be put on display in the hope this would encourage greater interest in meeting the war bonds quota. However, when the tank arrived, amid much excited anticipation, it was discovered not to be the real thing but a cheap replica. Stockport folk immediately lost interest and the tank languished on display for a short while before being quietly taken away again. The local paper dismissed it as 'a piece of comedy that has come and gone which has upset the town's dignity'. The council glossed over this unfortunate episode by issuing a list of American war maxims that it felt might be helpful to the war effort:

- eat less; breathe more
- talk less; think more
- ride less; walk more
- clothe less; bathe more
- worry less; work more
- waste less; give more
- preach less; practise more

It was subsequently arranged for a real tank to visit the town, but Stockport council declined the offer on the grounds that the impetus had been lost. Stockport Businessmen's Week failed to raise its target to purchase a battle cruiser and interest in war bonds declined still further.

Mrs Amy Saxon, who had been the mayor's secretary at the town hall for two years, had been appointed the chief executive officer of the Stockport food control committee. The committee issued guidelines on how to prepare economical dishes, but there were also 130 orders issued in formal and difficult official language that left many folk uncertain as to exactly what was required. The first communal kitchen was now being set-up and meat rationing came into force on 25 March. Rationing in general, however, got off to a bad start and there were inadequate supplies of tea and margarine.

Small shopkeepers had to have a minimum of 112 customers per week registered for 4oz (about 125g) of margarine so that their wholesale requirements would be at least 28lb (around 12.5kg). Unless this happened they would not be allowed to sell margarine. Stockport was described as an urban district and was allotted 7 tons of margarine, but Mrs Saxon insisted it was a county borough and requested 12 tons.

The council had now organised a municipal food depot from which food could be distributed. During the previous eighteen months the number of allotments had risen from seventeen to 1,276, but Stockport Smallholdings and Allotment Committee aimed to have 2,000 allotment holders in the town and were arranging to take over another 25 acres of land for this purpose. Allotment growers were asked to grow a variety of vegetables including onions, sweetcorn, haricot beans, peas, and beetroot, as well as potatoes, and they were now encouraged to raise ducks as 'flesh food'. The *Stockport Advertiser* was full of hints on potato-growing and poultry-hatching methods, and carrots were heavily promoted for multiple uses as soup, vegetable and pudding. Official arrangements were made for the marketing of surplus produce.

Farmers were mainly concentrating on growing potatoes or grain crops. Government guidelines indicated that 100 acres could produce:

- sufficient potatoes to feed 400 people for one year
- sufficient wheat to feed 230 people for one year
- sufficient barley to feed 180 people for one year
- sufficient oats to feed 150 people for one year
- sufficient beef grazing to feed 15 people for one year

The cost of living had now risen over 100% and gas and electricity costs were due to rise by a further 10% in mid-April. Easter was a cold, wet, miserable time. Gas for use in cars was banned and petrol was banned for 'frivolous journeys'. Both food and travel restrictions put a further dampener on things. The cotton workers and the hatters took their Easter holidays as usual from Maundy Thursday through to the following Tuesday, and the engineering shops were mostly closed, but the munitions workers were allowed no time off at all. The engineers were threatening to strike for better pay and conditions, but it was hoped that the critical situation on the Western Front would deter them.

There was a reduced London train service from 1 April (Easter Monday) to save coal and the 'permanent way' (i.e. track maintenance) plus the speeds of express or 'fast' trains were also subject to reduction. The hatting trade was badly affected by the Manpower Bill. In the manufacture of silk hats the exemptions of all classes of workmen in Grade 1 from 1875 were to be terminated. Similarly wool/felt and fur/felt foremen, proofers and dyers from 1883 and all remaining classes of workmen within the hatting trade from 1875. All fit men in the hatting trade up to the age of 42 had already been taken and the trade was only carrying on with the older male and female workers.

There were rate rises to cope with paying war bonuses to corporation employees and controversy still raged over the new education bill and its impact on factory working hours with the introduction of compulsory education for youngsters between the ages of 14 – 18 and the abolition of half-timers. This was to stop young teenagers taking unskilled dead-end jobs that would not last, or exhausting themselves by trying to attend school and undertaking employment. Skilled workers would be needed to replace those lost in the war. Many mills and manufactories relied on young, cheap labour and did not wish to pay adult rates. Newsagents were also prohibited from employing paperboys, although this measure was deferred until after the war was over. One piece of good news was that there were to be higher pensions for children and orphans, although it was little enough on which to keep them.

- 1st child would now receive 6s 8d (£14.49) formerly 5s (£10.88)
- 2nd child would now receive 5s (£10.88) formerly 4s 2d (£9.05)
- 3rd child would now receive 4s 2d (£9.05) formerly 3s 4d (£7.27)
- All others would now receive 4s 2d (£9.05) formerly 2s 6d (£5.44)

The bureaucracy involved in what would now be termed the 'benefits system' was cumbersome and confusing, so the *Stockport Advertiser* ran a weekly column of advice on war pensions and allowances. Conditions for receipt of benefits were constantly changing and, in spring 1918, an updated definition of entitlements and groups was published to clarify matters:

- PoWs: wife and dependents were to receive allowances as before
- Farm workers: no allowances other than wages
- Sergeant's wife: 15/- (£32.64) if she had no children + sergeant's 'allotment' of 5s 10d (£12.70)
- Husband's death: funeral grant if he died at home
- Insurance for discharged soldiers: 10/- (£21.76) per week; or 5/- per week (£10.88) if receiving disablement benefit
- Home Service enlistments: this included anyone not on military service who reached minimum height requirements for various occupations and allowances were paid according to individual circumstances
- Dependent's allowance: additional allowances could be made according to individual circumstances
- Hospital stoppages: serving soldiers received no extra allowance, just their pay; pensioned soldiers would receive extra allowances for wives and children
- Training allowances: no allowances while discharged soldiers wait for re-training
- Separation allowance: allowance for private's wife with four children under 14 and one over 14 is 33/- (£71.79) per week
- Local war pensions: may make allowances of dependant/s unable to work but have property responsibilities
- Hospitalised allowances: 20s 6d (£44.59) for a soldier; 13s 9d (£29.93) for his wife; 9s 2d (£19.93) for two young children

A major piece of news on the Home Front in early 1918 was that on 8 February the Representation of the People's Bill became an Act and therefore the law of the land. Women over the age of 30 now had the vote and fresh voters' lists would have to be prepared. The new voters' register for Stockport was expected to contain at least 50,000 names. This was in sharp contrast to 1914 when there had only been 13,380 eligible voters, and the last electoral roll had contained 25,171 names. The six month residency qualification for being eligible to vote would end on 15 April, although the vote for men could be conferred by occupation of business premises in the constituency with a certain yearly value (i.e. rent, rates and taxes paid) of £10 (about £435) for each voter. Tenants, landlords and owners could also vote and appeals could be made for anomalies. Men had to be over 21 to vote. Women had to be over the age of 30 on 15 April 1918 and needed residential qualifications or a house with at least a £5 (around £218) yearly value. Lodgers were allowed to vote, but only if they were male.

Although occupation was the basic criteria, it seemed that this was open to 'complicated interpretation'. Naval and military personnel could vote as well. Men had to be aged 19 and women had to be aged 30, and there was also a 'one month in the services' qualification necessary. The new parliamentary borough of Stockport was 'co-terminous' with the municipal borough. Revision courts were abolished and a town clerk was appointed. Registration forms were sent out and voters' lists prepared, printed and published by 16 June. The new register would come into operation by 1 October 1918. There were just five grounds for voter disqualification:

- aliens
- conscientious objectors
- those born with mental problems
- prisoners
- those disqualified for corrupt/illegal election practices

When the new lists were finally drawn up there were over 60,000 voters in Stockport, of whom 24,630 were women.

Stockport's investment in its war bonds quota remained low. Stockport Guardians (who looked after the workhouse) pleaded that they could not afford to invest in war bonds. Flag days were held on 3 and 4 May in Stockport as part of a special appeal for the Stockport YMCA hut week. In total the hut week raised nearly £3,500 (£1,232,000). A number of YMCA huts had been destroyed in the

Somme area due to heavy fighting. Charity events and concerts were held on a regular basis. One of the more unusual charity events was a 'butterfly day' (when butterfly 'favours' were purchased) in aid of the local RSPCA fund for sick and wounded horses at the Front, and this raised almost £800 (£281,500). Flag days, charity events and the PoWs' food/comforts parcels fund were well-supported, but there was still a marked reluctance on the part of individuals and organisations to invest in government war bonds. The attention and efforts of most people were focused on the food and fuel shortages and on eking out the supplies they were allowed under rationing restrictions, although in April there was the unexpected treat of a glut of bacon for the town. Flour could only be sold in four different measured weights in accordance with the orders of the food controllers, and folk were urged not to use flour in home cooking. Cakes and biscuits were in very short supply and often non-existent. Choices of fresh fruit and vegetables were limited in the winter months since only home-grown produce could be supplied. Porridge was the almost universal breakfast. However, food rationing had disbanded the endless queues for groceries and ensured a much more equal distribution of foodstuffs. A weekly list of food rations per adult was published and, although slightly inadequate in terms of quantity, it was more than adequate in terms of quality, to the extent that the rationing eradicated all the diseases of malnutrition, notably rickets and scurvy. A century later the disease of rickets has returned together with epidemics of diabetes and obesity. It is ironic that the cure seemingly lies in a 100-year-old diet adopted during a time of war. Local allotment growers were advised to grow Golden Wonder, Langworthy and Windsor Castle potatoes, as they had the best flavour, and there was also encouragement to grow carrots, other root crops, haricot beans, onions, spinach, and tomatoes.

To Stockport's great pride, the Cheshires were mentioned in dispatches for acts of great gallantry on the battlefield and soldiers from the town were awarded a number of different medals.

It was a bright moment in a generally very bleak time. The Armoury also announced that it had entertained over 205,000 wounded soldiers

Amiens on the Somme c1917

during the war years. The budget had not proved too burdensome, because the war had temporarily virtually abolished unemployment which, in turn, was responsible for higher wages. Although prices had risen as well, there had been a certain redistribution of wealth. However, beer, tobacco and tea duty was increased in the 1918 budget, a measure that in some way affected almost everyone. There was also a rate increase in Stockport of 1s 4d (£2.92) in the pound, accompanied by a breakdown of expenditure. Committee overspends were mainly due to increased costs of wages, materials and interest rates. Finance (due to the cost of the new registration lists) and Education (due to rises in teachers' wages) had the largest increases. The gas department was now returning no profits, although the electricity department had given the same small return as in 1917 and the trams had given £500 (£21,750) more profit. The rates expenditure was divided between four main areas: borough; improvement; general district; and poor rate (Guardians and Overseers). Street repairs, housing maintenance and sewage renewal works were all cut back. The health department announced further progress for medical treatments for schoolchildren suffering from physical defects who had been unable to benefit fully from education.

Nearly half of the town's schoolchildren had some kind of problem. The ultimate goal was their future contribution to the country because the nation would require 'physically and mentally efficient children to win supremacy after the war'. At the same time, education was made to 'suffer patriotically' so that Stockport schoolboys could 'provide service on the land'. Stockport Grammar School and the municipal secondary school were expected to provide sizeable contingents of boys. So far, 17,000 lads were required for work on the land and numbers of 'lasses' were also urgently required. The government had finally succeeded in squashing the resistance of Cheshire farmers to women working on the land. Indeed, many of the farmers now confessed themselves pleasantly surprised by the abilities and hard work of their female farmhands.

As if to celebrate this new-found liberal awareness, Stockport Theatre Royal staged *Hindle Wakes*. The play was very daring for the times. Written in 1910 by Stanley Houghton, it tells the story of a young mill girl who has an illicit weekend away with the son of the mill owner for whom she works. Despite much opposition, the boy wants to marry her but, to everyone's horror, she refuses. She likes the boy but she does not love him. Her family disown her but she is confident that her skills as a weaver will allow her to support herself as an independent woman. The play was first performed in 1912 and was so controversial that Oxford University students were banned by their vice chancellor from seeing it. Despite this concern with 'modern female morals', the play toured for over seven years and was much enjoyed by many Stockport folk.

The need for men to replace the 'cannon fodder' on the Western Front was becoming ever more desperate. In nearby Altrincham, a hospital was opened for treating troops suffering from shell-shock, which was then a little-understood phenomenon. In Stockport, medical examinations of older men called-up was placing a severe strain on the Medical Board situated in the old free library in the market place. The volunteers asked for 15,000 Grade 2 men for two or three months to be spent on Home Front defence work. The casualty lists continued to grow, however, and the merchant navy continued to take a pounding

DISCOVER MORE ABOUT MILITARY HISTORY

Pen & Sword Books have over 4000 books currently available, our imprints include; Aviation, Naval, Military, Archaeology, Transport, Frontline, Seaforth and the Battleground series, and we cover all periods of history on land, sea and air.

Keep up to date with our new releases by completing and returning the form below (no stamp required if posting in the UK).

Alternatively, if you have access to the internet, please complete your details online via our website at **www.pen-and-sword.co.uk.**

All those subscribing to our mailing list via our website will receive a free e-book, *Mosquito Missions* by Martin W Bowman. Please enter code number ACC1 when subscribing to receive your free e-book.

Mr/Mrs/Ms ....

Address..

....

Postcode................................. Email address..

Website: www.pen-and-sword.co.uk Email: enquiries@pen-and-sword.co.uk
Telephone: 01226 734555   Fax: 01226 734438
Stay in touch: facebook.com/penandswordbooks or follow us on Twitter @penswordbooks

2

Freepost Plus RTKE-RGRJ-KTTX
Pen & Sword Books Ltd
47 Church Street
BARNSLEY
S70 2AS

Greek Street School Military Hospital, Stockport c1918

as its ships desperately tried to reach Britain with supplies of food, arms and raw materials. Although food shortages were at times severe in Britain, the country never reached famine or starvation point. Stockport in particular appreciated the sailors' efforts and, despite not being a coastal town, set up a branch of the British and Foreign Sailors Association.

Farmers became alarmed at the prospect that another 30,000 men would be taken from agriculture and were promptly criticised as absolutely selfish in not wanting their own sons to go to war while everyone else's sons had to go. The authorities assured them that farm labourers called-up would be replaced because food production was of vital importance for the country. In addition, recruitment meetings for the Women's Land Army were going well.

The munitions industry was also badly hit by the new call-up regulations but, to everyone's surprise, former domestic servants looking for work showed great aptitude and became proficient in a number of different technical jobs in the munitions industry. Compromises were made in the new education bill to free up working potential. The clause that 'attendance at continuation schools over the four years from 14 – 18 with 320 hours each year' was amended to 'attendance for two years from 14-16 with 600 hours per year', then subsequently the hours for 14 – 16 year olds were reduced to 280 hours per annum, and attendance from 16 – 18 was no longer compulsory.

Cold winds in May and June badly affected the blossom on the trees and there were warnings of a bad fruit harvest. Consequently, the jam ration was cut from 4oz (about 125g) to 1oz (around 30g). Lectures were given in Stockport on fruit preserving and how to bottle fruit and vegetables. The Smallholdings and Allotment Committee opened a canning department in the showrooms of the gas offices in Portwood so that folk could take their fruit and vegetables to be canned at minimal cost, i.e. 4d (74p) for a 2lb (1kg) can. New ration books were issued on 14 July with different coloured pages for sugar, meat, bacon, butter, margarine and tea. Tea and meat rations were increased slightly, but lard was now added to rationed foodstuffs. Amazingly, at least 2,000 applications for ration books gave no address.

Gas prices had risen again and Stockport's first municipal kitchen opened in Portwood. There were complaints about the quality of frozen meat in Stockport. Local butchers refused to accept frozen meat and the local inspector of food condemned it as unfit for human consumption. This did much to counteract the action of officials issuing the meat whose basic attitude was 'take it or leave it'.

There were continuing problems with the prices, supply and distribution of milk and a scheme to nationalise milk supplies was suggested to eradicate the ongoing problems. Cheshire farmers had finally agreed on minimum wages and working hours. All able-bodied males over the age of 18 would be paid 36/- (£78.31) for a six day/sixty hour working week and females would receive 25/- (£54.38) for the same amount of work. Overtime would be paid at an extra rate, with more on Sundays, and the hourly rate would nearly double during the hay and corn harvests.

There was now also a war work volunteers' scheme in operation. It was a scheme for men of the 'new military age' (i.e. aged up to 51) under which middle-aged men who did voluntary war work, such as in agriculture, might not be called-up, and those over 45 in Grade 1 and those over 35 in Grade 2 categories were eligible. The agricultural wages were low and within months there was a threatened strike by male agricultural workers for a fifty-five-hour week and a basic minimum wage of 42/- (£91.36).

There had been whooping cough and measles epidemics in Stockport and at the end of June it was noted that there was also an influenza epidemic. A number of cases were reported but seemed to be mild although highly infectious with symptoms of shivering, sickness, back and joint pain. Local schools closed due to this epidemic and the town's 'baby week' was postponed. This strain of influenza was particularly virulent because it was a hybrid of pig flu and human flu.

It was a busy summer supporting the war effort and war charities. The mayor handed over £3614 (£157,200) to Stockport YMCA hut fund. Heaton Moor, Heaton Chapel and Heaton Mersey between them raised just over £2,000 (about £87,000) for the infirmary extension fund, and the open air music festival in Vernon Park also raised money for the infirmary. Stockport Vocal Union gave madrigal concerts. The Red Cross raised cash through local bowling matches to pay for hospital staff and equipment, and the local boy scouts played cricket at Cale Green to support war charities. The Red Cross were also undertaking a national collection of gold and silver gifts to celebrate the silver wedding of King George V and Queen Mary on 8 July. Some felt this was perhaps a little excessive. The war had seen a rise in weddings as couples hastened to marry while they could still have the chance of a little snatched happiness, but the keywords of most of these war weddings were economy and austerity. While folk wished the king and queen well, it was suggested that such gold and silver should really go towards the war effort. The king, who was anxious to show that 'we are all in this together', had insisted on the same rations for the royal family as everyone else, would doubtless have agreed.

The taking up of war bonds in the town was improved by Bonar

Parish Church, Stockport c1918

Law's initiative in reducing the deposit rate to 3% so that folk got 2½% more income from bonds than from money on deposit. Lloyd George had always maintained that the war was as much about business interests as about principles, and this response seemed to prove his point. For the first two years of the war, from 1914 – 1916, Stockport Soldiers and Sailors Family Association had had the responsibility for paying pensions and allowances to soldiers, sailors and their dependents and had paid out a total of £10,500 (£635,800). From 1916 – 1918, the Stockport War Pensions Committee had taken over responsibility and, to date, had paid out £16,000 (£696,100).

Having spent much of the war criticising the local Labour MP, George Wardle, for his politics, the *Stockport Advertiser* came to his rescue in late June after he and other Labour MPs had been forced to issue a public manifesto protesting against sniping and attacks from their own side. The paper criticised those responsible as 'anti-national fictionalists' and condemned 'socialists and the rabid ILP' for 'pulling down' their elected MPs. It didn't last long. Three weeks later the

Advertiser undertook some extensive pre-electioneering for the Conservative candidate, Sir Henry Norris, and urged all Labour Party members to dissociate themselves from Ramsay McDonald because he was 'unfit to represent any body of Englishmen'. The National Union of Railwaymen (NUR) now decided to withdraw their support for Mr Wardle, a move that he condemned as 'contrary to the rules and practice of democracy'. The reasons for the NUR's actions are unclear but appear to stem from annoyance that Mr Wardle did not consult them as to his every parliamentary action. The *Advertiser* could not resist adding its own comments that 'the Labour Party in Stockport, with its pacifists and Bolsheviks and various factions, is in a hopeless tangle'. Mr Wardle eventually withdrew his nomination from the NUR and stood as an Independent candidate.

The fourth anniversary of the war was coming up and it had been decided that elections, parliamentary and municipal, should be held in October. This was later amended to December after the war had actually ended. A day of remembrance was held on 4 August and an intersession Sunday was held on 6 August at the request of the king. The paper devoted much comment to the war's anniversary before taking the Labour Party to task once more and finally commenting that 'the price of liberty is eternal vigilance'.

By now there was a sense that perhaps the end of the war really was in sight as Allied victories began to replace Allied defeats. Christies' hat-works increased their subscription fivefold to Stockport's promotion of the 'Feed the Guns' campaign. The Ring Spinning Company invested £25,000 (£8,798,000) in war bonds. There was also an extensive recruitment campaign for Queen Mary's Army Auxiliary Corps, advertising for 30,000 women to undertake clerical and driving duties, cooking, waitressing and domestic work. Women were now being sent to France to relieve the men of non-combatant duties so they could fight at the Front.

A lighter note was introduced by the realisation that the women would need to learn some of the slang terms that the men used to refer to various items or actions. A 'barker' was a sausage, stemming from the fact that the troops believed their sausages were made from dog meat, while the term 'sausage' was used for observation balloons. Porridge was 'burgoo', bread was 'rooti', jam was 'possy', cheese was 'bung' and an 'egg' was not something laid by a hen but slang for a hand-grenade. The meaning of words can change with time and nowhere is this more evident than with the verb 'to bonk' which, in the First World War, meant to shell with artillery fire.

A Household Fuel Requisitioning Order had come into force and fuel allowances could be taken in gas, coal or coke. Fuel rationing forms were to be completed and handed in at the town hall. Coke was a good and much cheaper substitute for coal. Gas was not encouraged for domestic lighting. If annual need did not exceed 22,500 cubic feet of gas for lighting and fuel, or 65cwt of coal and coke, no requisition order was needed. Household fuel allowances were determined as:

1 ton of coal OR 1.5 tons coke OR 15,000 cubic feet of gas OR 800B of trade units of electricity.

Gas and coke were the preferred fuels as that meant a 25% saving in coal resources, mining labour and necessary transport facilities. There were 25,000 fuel requisition order forms issued with full details of fuel types, dealers and dwellings. Coal cellars were inspected by the local fuel overseers and any existing stocks could affect rations. Theatres, music halls and other places of entertainment were to reduce their fuel and lighting by 25%.

Newspapers, periodicals, and magazines were collected, often by the boy scouts, for recycling and for economy, as there was a paper shortage crisis. A salvage scheme for collecting and re-using tin cans was suggested. Men's old suits were requisitioned, and the price of new ones rose, as the government undertook to clothe and re-fit US troops in Europe in return for food supplies.

The shortage of raw materials and higher costs were a problem, especially for wool. Between June and October 1917, the government had contracts for 31,000,000 yards (28,210,000m) of khaki cloth 56 inches (1.42m) wide, while £1 (£43.51) per yard (0.91 m) was paid for grey suitings and £1.10s (£65.26) for good blue serges. The war, according to one politician, had taught everyone much about economy and recycling items and materials that previously had simply been 'rubbish heaps of potential wealth'.

Another million acres of arable land was needed and a new home agriculture programme was drawn up in Cheshire for 1919. Food resources had improved with rationing and, while January to March had been lean months, partly due to the natural agricultural and climatic cycles, it was felt that drastic shortages should not recur. Allotment holders were urged to grow leeks, celery and vegetable marrows and a bumper Cheshire harvest of wheat, oats and barley was forecast. Shoppers still paid five- or six-times pre-war prices for peas and vegetables, but now there was virtually no profiteering and folk accepted that fewer supplies and the cost of the war were the reasons rather than someone's personal greed and selfishness.

Many allotment holders also kept chickens and each week the local paper published hints for successful poultry yards. It was advised that cockerels should, by and large, not be kept, as they did not produce eggs but still required feeding. A few were needed for fertilisation purposes, but most cockerels ended up on the butcher's stalls after a rather brief life. The government relaxed regulations on killing birds and most species could now be shot for the pot. The rearing of rabbits was encouraged to increase the meat supply. Rabbit meat was popular until the mid-twentieth century, but the taste is too strong for most modern palates and it has gone out of fashion along with the heads, tongues and offal of sheep and cattle.

Milk prices were still a problem and there were diminished milk supplies in some areas of Stockport. Before the war the cost of a milk cow had been £20 (£870) and now it was about four-times that amount. The price of winter feeding stuffs had also risen. Consequently, the prices of butter and cheese had risen sharply, but milk was still 7d (£1.26) a quart (just under 1 litre). The local food controller therefore agreed a new fixed price of 9d (£1.65) a quart.

The coal rationing forms caused confusion and delays because many were not returned. It was essential that Form 2 was sent to the coal dealers and Form 3 to the town hall for proper regulation and distribution of supplies. However, there was a number of claims, counter claims and anomalies to be considered. Claims for excess quantities of coal were deferred simply due to the coal deficit. Classes of 'early start' workers, schools, the elderly and infirm could apply for extra rations, but there simply wasn't sufficient coal.

The housing situation in Stockport was grim. The decline in house-building was almost total. In 1913 333 new houses were built in the borough. In 1917 just five new houses were built, four in Edgeley and one in Shaw Heath. This hardly constituted the 'land fit for heroes' troops had been promised after the war.

There was another problem looming as well, which was much more serious and this was employment. Many soldiers and sailors expected to return to the jobs that they had held before the war, but this was clearly not going to be the case. Although there had been an increase in the volume of work, female employees and juvenile placements had filled the vacancies. Engineering apprentice classes were held on Saturday mornings in the technical school. The munitions industry would scale down once the war was over.

Although the Ring Spinning and the Broadstone Spinning companies in Stockport had been quite successful during the war, the cotton and hatting industries were generally in decline for various reasons, and the engineering industry was looking for people with up-to-date skills and knowledge. It was clear that employers were going to be hesitant about 'taking on khaki over skills and experience'.

Stockport Corporation was going to have few extra financial resources after paying war bonuses to its employees. The current cost was £24,500 (£8,622,000) for 900 non-certified employees. This amount would be doubled if certified employees were included, and there was now pressure to do so.

The tide of the war had turned and by mid-October the Allies were having a number of successes in the final 'hundred days offensive' of the war. Bunting and Union Jacks flew in the town. Sergeant Thomas Watson, one of ten brothers in the army and a member of Stockport borough police force, was awarded the DCM for gallantry. Germany was 'on the brink' of accepting the armistice conditions laid down by

President Wilson of the United States, which caused much excitement in the town but also raised many concerns as to what would happen when all the troops eventually returned to 'Blighty'.

The mayor, Mr Rowbotham, was still appealing for war funds and gave a public address in Stockport on 1 November. Afterwards, a small girl came up to him and placed 4d (74p) in his hand, which she said was to help with the war. Touched, the mayor placed her contribution in an envelope and sent it directly to Andrew Bonar Law, then chancellor of the exchequer. Bonar Law wrote back to the child saying that he 'greatly appreciated her patriotic action'.

The British finally broke through German defences during the battle of the Hindenburg Line on 17 October. After that things happened fast. The Eastern Front capitulated after losing the lengthy battle of Sharon and the British captured Damascus. Bulgaria signed an armistice with the Allies and the once mighty Ottoman Empire followed suit. Croatia, Serbia and Slovenia proclaimed their own state, which became colloquially known as Yugoslavia. Austria-Hungary made peace with Italy, then the Austrian kaiser, Charles, abdicated and Austria was proclaimed a republic. Czechoslovakia became a republic two days later. Finally, Germany admitted defeat. Kaiser Wilhelm abdicated and 'at the eleventh hour on the eleventh day of the eleventh month', Germany signed the Armistice of Compiegne. The Great War was finally over.

There was 'delirious joy' and relief in Stockport. Now the Cheshires would return to claim their colours from St Georges' church. The Cheshire Volunteer battalions, including the 8th Stockport Battalion, the Territorials, and all those who had survived the dreadful carnage, both on land and at sea, would finally return home. Peace nights were held in theatres and there were thanksgiving services in churches. The celebrations were tinged with sadness for those who would never come home, but Christmas 1918 would truly be a time of joy and goodwill for the first time in five years.

The 'evening gowns and small satin hats' that had taken up column inches in the *Advertiser* at the end of October could now come into their own. There would still be rationing. Trade routes and sources of food and raw materials needed to be re-established. Business interests needed to be recreated. Workers needed to return to the mines, the fields and factories in full force. The war had taken a terrible toll on both lives and livelihoods, and the cost had been beyond incredible. There were also those who fondly imagined that now hostilities had ceased the old order would be restored and life would continue as it had before.

That would never happen. The Great War had crossed a line and destroyed a whole way of life. Nothing would ever be the same again.

List of Illustrations

❖

Buxton Road, Stockport c1910.
St George's Church, Stockport c1914
Armoury Square, Shaw Heath c1914s
Town Hall, Stockport c1914
Wellington Road North, Stockport c1914
Naval battle of Falkland, Atlantic Ocean 1914
St George's Schools Military Hospital, Stockport c1915
Recruiting tram, Stockport c1915 (courtesy of Stockport Local
  Studies)
Stockport in the Great War c1915
Recruits returning from route march to the Armoury 15 June 1915
  (courtesy of Stockport Local Studies)
Western Front c1915
Cheshire farmers near Great Moor, Stockport c1916
Shellfire in France c1916
Stockport Infirmary as a military hospital c1916
Stockport Technical School c1908
Buxton Road, Stockport c1913
Stockport Sunday School c1912
Land Army girls with Shire horses in Bramhall 1916 (courtesy of
  Stockport Local Studies)
Vernon Park, Stockport c1909
George Wardle, MP for Stockport c1915
Ward 2, Heaton Mersey Red Cross Hospital c1915 (courtesy of
  Stockport Local Studies)

Female workers drilling tank engine cylinders at Mirrlees c1918
  (courtesy of Stockport Local Studies)
Amiens on the Somme c1917
Greek Street School Military Hospital, Stockport c1918
Parish Church, Stockport c1918

Index